Culture, Development, and Public Administration in Africa

Culture, Development, and Public Administration in Africa

Ogwo J. Umeh and Greg Andranovich
with Foreword by Jong S. Jun

Kumarian
Press, Inc.

Culture, Development, and Public Administration in Africa
Published in 2005 in the United States of America by Kumarian Press, Inc.,
1294 Blue Hills Avenue, Bloomfield, CT 06002 USA

The text of this book is set in Giovanni

Production and design by The Agrell Group, Lewis@theagrellgroup.com
Proofread by Pat Althoen

Printed in the U.S.A. by Thomson-Shore, Inc., Dexter, MI.

The paper used in this publication meets the minimum requirements of the American
National Standard for Information Sciences—Permanence of Paper for Printed Library
Materials, ANSI Z39.48-1984

Library of Congress Cataloging-in-Publication Data
Umeh, Ogwo J., 1952-
Culture, development, and public administration in Africa /
    Ogwo J. Umeh and Greg Andranovich.
        p. cm.

Summary: "This book illustrates the need to incorporate local cultural
dynamics into international development and public administration programs
where Western models dominate. Examples include South Africa, Botswana,
Lesotho, Malawi, Swaziland, Tanzania, Zambia, and Zimbabwe. The authors, an
American political scientist and an African public administration professor,
write for undergraduate and graduate students, as well as for policymakers,
managers, and administrators"--Provided by publisher.
        Includes bibliographical references and index.
        ISBN 1-56549-201-3 (pbk. : alk. paper) -- ISBN 1-56549-200-5 (cloth : alk. paper)
1. Public administration--Africa--Case studies. 2. Africa--Politics and
    government--Case studies. 3. Political culture--Africa. 4. National
    characteristics, African. 5. Africa--Social conditions. 6. Economic
    development. I. Andranovich, Gregory. II. Title.
JQ1890.U64 2005
    353.7'0968--dc22

                                                            2004027580

---

14 13 12 11 10 09 08 07 06 05   10 9 8 7 6 5 4 3 2 1   First Printing 2005

DEDICATION

To David, Lisa and Jessica Umeh for their understanding and patience while this book project was being completed

and

To the wild bunch—Andrew, Alex, Haley, Eva and David— for a better tomorrow.

Contents

FIGURES

SOUTHERN AFRICA

NEA

alabo
Douala
Yaounde
Bangui
Bata
Libreville
GABON
CONGO
Brazzaville
Pointe-Noire
Kinshasa
Cabinda
(ANGOLA)
Luanda
ZAIRE
Kisangani
Lake Albert
UGANDA
Kampala
KENYA
Mogadishu
Lake Victoria
Nairobi
RWANDA
Kigali
BURUNDI
Bujumbura
Kananga
Kalemie
TANZANIA
Mombasa
Dar es Salaam
Lake Tanganyika
Mbeya
Kasama
ANGOLA
Lobito
Luena
Lubumbashi
MALAWI
Lake Nyasa
Kitwe
Lilongwe
Nacala
Namibe
ZAMBIA
Lusaka
Lake Kariba
Mahajang
Antananarivo
Harare
MOZAMBIQUE
NAMIBIA
Windhoek
ZIMBABWE
Bulawayo
Beira
MADAGASCAR
BOTSWANA
Toliara
SOUTH AFRICA
(Walvis Bay)
Luderitz
Gaborone
Pretoria
Johannesburg
Maputo
Mbabane
SWAZILAND
Maseru
LESOTHO
Durban
SOUTH AFRICA
Cape Town
Port Elizabeth

University of Alabama, Cartographic Research Lab

Foreword

In the past, comparative public administration focused on the exploration of similarities and differences in structure, functions, and processes among countries, using Western theories and approaches. The tacit assumption underlying comparative study was that public administration in Western countries was rational, functionally efficient, and professionally competent, and hence could be used as a model for cross-cultural comparison. When a Western framework was used in comparative research, however, various social and cultural elements unique to any non-Western country were left out. Realizing this limitation in recent years, scholars have employed an interpretive approach, seeking the hidden dimensions of political and administrative contexts. To truly understand the problems and uniqueness of a country, comparative research needs to reflect the changing conditions of society, including its political, cultural, and socioeconomic aspects. When these dynamic aspects are neglected, development policies inevitably produce various unintended consequences in their implementation.

Because southern African countries strive for modernization and development, it is important that they develop an efficient and effective institutional capability in order to improve their projects. Public administration practitioners assert that non-Western countries should learn Western methods in order to improve their administration. This assertion, however, is true only up to a point. Western ways of managing public institutions and their role in social change and development are superior to those of less industrialized countries in many ways. But development policies and administration in African countries are value laden, and the cultural norms of each country are constituted by its historical, cultural, and social traditions. Values and cultural norms in different administrative settings are numerous, flexible, hidden, changing, and intersecting. Because they are influenced by various factors, they cannot easily be understood through the scientific research method by applying Western theories and concepts. Language and symbols express the values and meanings embedded in administrative culture and people's experiences. Thus in order to discover the meanings underlying the successes and failures of development policies, we need to interpret and understand qualitative and quantitative information, stories and cases, communication, and the experiences of individuals in different administrative settings.

The authors of *Culture, Development, and Public Administration in Africa*, Ogwo Jombo Umeh and Greg Andranovich, explore local cultures and their influence on southern African development. They offer invaluable lessons for improving the development process by emphasizing the linkages among culture, values, politics, and bureaucracy, and by critiquing the available statistical information.

Culture is easier to talk about than to define. The authors view culture as "the system of values, symbols, and shared meanings of a group, including the embodiment of these values, symbols, and meanings into material objects and ritualized practices." Every administrative system is influenced by the greater culture, whether the greater culture is democratic or autocratic in its governance. In order to change policy and administrative processes, we must understand the political, historical, and cultural contexts in which they have arisen.

I believe that more interpretive and cross-cultural research focusing on culture and development will lead us to locally practical knowledge, which is exceedingly useful to an understanding of human issues in development. The internationalization movement will, ideally, be built on the participation of, and interdependence among, government organizations, businesses, civic organizations, groups, and citizens both locally and globally. Ineluctably, the process will involve critical discourse and dialogue: both are necessary for socially constructing the meaning of development and human action. Comparative development administration needs to reflect not only the historical, social, economic, and cultural aspects of a country's development, but also the problems and processes of global interconnectedness.

Jong S. Jun
Hayward, CA

Acknowledgments

We are indebted to many for their assistance in reading our manuscript, in whole or part, and for making invaluable suggestions and editorial comments. We would like to thank everyone who offered comments on earlier versions of the manuscript: Jong S. Jun for writing the Foreword and the University of Alabama's Cartographic Research Lab for the use of their map of Africa. Special thanks also goes to Richard Vengroff who provided the inspiration to venture into the comparative and development administration field. We are greatly indebted to the reviewers selected by Kumarian Press, Robert Dibie and others, for their constructive reviews and suggestions. And, most significantly, we would like to thank Krishna Sondhi (Publisher), Jim Lance (Editor), and other staff members at Kumarian Press for their dedication and support in completing this book.

Acronyms

ANC—African National Congress
CAG—Comparative Administration Group
CAR—Central African Republic
CCM—Chama Cha Mapinduzi
CIN—Culture in the Neighborhood
COSATU—Congress of South African Trade Unions
EEA—Ethiopian Economic Association
GEAR—Growth, Employment And Redistribution
HIPC—Heavily Indebted Poor Countries
IDASA—Institute for a Democratic Alternative South Africa
IOC—International Olympic Committee
MFDP—Ministry of Finance and Development Planning
MLGLH—Ministry of Local Government, Land and Housing
NASPAA—National Association of Schools of Public Affairs and
Administration
NCOP—National Council of Provinces
RDP—Reconstruction and Development Program
SADC—South African Development Community
SADCC—South African Development Coordinating Conference
SAMDI—South African Management Development Institute
SMS—Senior Management Service
TANU—Tanganyika African Union
ULGS—Unified Local Government Services
USAID—United States Agency for International Development
ZAPU—Zimbabwe African National Union

Chapter One

Introduction

O ne of the stark realities in the twenty-first century is that people need government. Oftentimes, the abilities of people to articulate their demands are not matched by the capacities of governments to provide security and public services. Increasingly, as people demand a stake in their future, the initial task of the state is to simultaneously provide services and conduct nation-building. Yet in country after country, in case after case, efforts in both service provision and nation-building are hard fought and the results seem less than spectacular. Are expectations too high? Are the conditions on the ground too tough? Why do the challenges of public administration in developing countries seem to be insurmountable?

In this book, we argue that the absence of a culturally sensitive orientation in conceptualizing and analyzing administrative management presents limitations that undermine how we research and evaluate findings within and across countries. We begin our inquiry with a critical assessment of prevailing models and frameworks used to explain the dynamics of public administration from a comparative perspective, and then present an interpretive approach that we believe adds a missing ingredient back into the mix. Then, we apply this interpretive approach to further explain a comprehensive set of responses on administrative and managerial tasks reported by public officials across the region of southern Africa. But this is getting ahead of our presentation.

By way of general introduction, this chapter first surveys the literature on the study of politics and public administration in Africa. Then we discuss the rationale for using an interpretive perspective. The third part of the chapter provides an overview of public administration in the African context. The chapter closes with brief profiles of the southern African countries that are the focus of the book.

Challenges in Contemporary Africa

Analyses of contemporary sub-Saharan African affairs paint a fairly dismal picture of the conditions of the people and the prospects for their economies and states (Chabal and Daloz 1999; Diamond and Plattner 1999; Harbeson 2000; Joseph 1998; Osabu-Kle 2000; Uzodike 1997). However, these same analysts have begun to probe more deeply the historical reasons for current challenges, and their findings are suggestive of a more complex reality in twenty-first century Africa south of the Sahara. A brief overview of their arguments, evidence, and suggestions provides a valuable introduction to the context within which we place our work. As a prelude, however, consider the remarks of the then-newly installed President of Uganda in an address at Dar es Salaam University in July 1986. His speech was entitled, "What's Wrong with Africa?" and he listed two primary reasons for the initial backwardness of the continent, first, the natural obstacles, such as deserts and topical forests, to the spread of ideas and commerce, and second, the climate ("which is a bit too comfortable"); a third reason that came later, was the "intrusion of foreign forces into the affairs of Africa" (Museveni 2000, 146-147; Kasfir 1999).

Recent scholarship on Africa focuses on these same challenges. Despite the relative success seen in the last years of the twentieth century, economic conditions in sub-Saharan Africa have deteriorated from the small but positive levels of growth in the decade following independence. These nations, for the most part, remain among the world's poorest (Callaghy 2000). Both the reasons for this and its consequences include national, regional, and global dimensions, and play an important explanatory role in the study of the emergence of democracy in African nations. At the level of the nation-state rapid population growth, increasing urbanization, weak agricultural output and the continuing food crisis, the inequality of women, and the ravaging effects of the AIDS crisis have contributed to ongoing economic problems and political challenges in these nations (Simmons 2001; World Bank 1989). Regional attempts to mitigate these problems have generally ended without success; the same difficulties that ensue elsewhere are problematic in Africa: perceptions of unequal gains, inadequate methods of compensation, ideological differences with regard to problem definition in policymaking, and the impact of foreign influences particularly with regard to aid and investment have undermined regional collaboration (Ojo 1985). Recent attempts at cooperation have either been functionally-oriented (such as in transportation, energy, health, or communication projects) or, as in the case of the Southern African Development Coordination Conference (reconstituted as SADC in 1992), have recognized the importance of the role of politics in establishing and maintaining regional relationships.

Globalization has marginalized much of sub-Saharan Africa. Nicholas van de Walle, summarizing the changing African political economy over the past two decades, concludes that the structural adjustment program put into effect by the World Bank did achieve some of its stated policy goals, such as simplifying tariff structures, establishing reasonable exchange rates, deregulating financial markets, and privatizing the parastatal sector. But the answer to the next question—what difference has this made?—is more complex. Donor support probably lessened the likelihood of real economic reform because African governments did not have to deal directly with the consequences of not attracting foreign capital investments in the 1980s and 1990s (van de Walle 2000, 276). Instead, these governments were able to continue to get money while not making any progress in reform. The results were increased indebtedness and a proliferation of donors and their institutional infrastructure in many nations, resulting in conditions of economic dependency (van de Walle 2000, 276). In the end, sub-Saharan Africa has remained marginalized in the world economy as the currents of globalization have become stronger.

At the same time, political analyses have addressed the changes that occurred in the transition toward democracy, including the public policies of western nations in support of free and fair elections, executive branch accountability, legislative branch professionalization, civil society strengthening, and a broadening of democratic values. For comparativists, elections—a sure signpost in the transition toward democracy—were the main focus of political analysis in the 1990s. Yet, as Goran Hyden has pointed out, neither the state nor the formal democratic processes are responsible for the lack of democracy and democratic practices. Quoting Michael Lofchie, Hyden reminds us that real authority is often not located in the institutional structure of the state: the importance of "informal and unofficial relations" in influencing political outcomes requires a broader framework for analysis (Hyden 1999, 182; Hyden, Olowu, and Okoth-Ogendo 2000). Given that the rules of politics are not those that are written, Hyden calls for a more nuanced analysis of African politics to include "the politics that surrounds the reconstitution of the political order in Africa" (183). Calling for the adoption of a governance focus, Hyden argues that there is now a need to shift the analytical lens away from the study of politics (who gets what, when, and how, as Harold Lasswell [1936] puts it) toward the examination of "issues related to the rules of the game...[or] 'constitutive politics'" (186).

Together, these dimensions point to the uses and management of power; that is, to the political context of democracy in southern Africa (Harbeson 2000). Crawford Young's conclusions about the third wave of democratization in Africa, for example, are derived through an examination of symbolic politics, particularly in how leaders in the 1990s have used the trappings of democracy (including freer presses, more respect for human rights, and contested elections) to navigate the "comprehensive superstructure of international accountability to which Africa is subject" (Young 1999, 34-35).

Young's conclusions might suggest that African leaders are playing a complicated game to remain in power, presenting themselves as part of a democratization movement to the international donor community while tightening their reigns domestically. How African leaders see themselves, and how they see the political system reflecting and shaping politics, are dimensions that need to be addressed in any assessment of democracy in Africa. U.O. Uzodike (1997, 28) notes that in many African societies, "traditional conceptions of democracy" focused on the group and emphasized the group over the individual. Current conflicts between such different roles in politics, society, and the economy are played out in the political economies of these nations. These conflicts are analyzed from the perspective of the legacy of colonial domination, which introduced the privileged role of the individual (and other capitalist ideas, such as property ownership) to these societies (Haugerud 1995). This new line of inquiry has also re-introduced the cultural basis for differences into the analysis of African politics.

One of the best examples of this line of inquiry is found in Daniel T. Osabu-Kle's *Compatible Cultural Democracy*, which makes the case for establishing a jaku democracy; jaku is the Ga word for "African." Osabu-Kle argues that understanding culture is the key to development in Africa, and that establishing culturally compatible political preconditions is different in Africa than it is in the West. He begins by differentiating between African and European politics. African politics is based on a culture of cooperation and compromise, where competition plays a destructive role (2000, 74-75). Prior to colonialism, the representation of different African clans on ruling councils at various levels in the political system provided opportunities for bargaining and reconciliation. Since colonialism and the founding of political parties on top of extant communal divisions within African societies, it has become much harder to create a climate for bargaining and reconciliation. Furthermore, given the different cultural bases for societal decision-making in Africa (valuing consensus rather than individualism, cooperation rather than competition), the circulation of elites is not as important as gaining the input of all elites (75).

Osabu-Kle discusses the different types of indigenous African political systems and argues that these fall into two main types (79). One type did not have a centralized authority, the administrative machinery to implement decisions, a centralized judicial system, or a sharp division in rank or social status. The second type, which was more prevalent, had a centralized authority, an administrative machinery, and a centralized judicial system. It utilized a hierarchical and concentric system of regions, zones, districts, towns, villages, and huts, to provide for the union of heterogeneous groups or clans. This political system worked to ensure the cohesion of the various groups or clans, and their capacity to pursue common interests (80). While the head of "state" was the territorial ruler, power was devolved to the subdivisions of the "state," where administrative and judicial functions were carried out. Given the enormous challenges of communication and transportation, the devolution of power served to check the central authority's powers (80).

At the local levels of this political system, the chiefs played a dual role. On the one hand they represented the interests of the local people when participating in decision-making outside of the region; on the other hand, the chiefs represented the central authority to the local people. The chiefs and the local councils balanced these two roles with the consent of the central authority and the consent of the local people.

Finally, Daniel Osabu-Kle notes that the role of leaders in this consensus-oriented political system went beyond the usual secular functions (80). As the embodiment of social and political values and mores, the leaders also reflected the mystical values of society. The importance of these mystical values and the symbols through which these values were held, played an important role in protecting against the abuse of political power, providing legitimacy to the exercise of power, and holding the political systems together through times of political crisis (80). Indeed, "these supernatural aspects of African rule—conditions that puzzled the Western mind—constituted an essential cohesive force that kept destructive centrifugal forces and abuse of power in check" (80-81).

The re-emergence of witchcraft and other mystical notions goes hand in hand with the transformation of the state and conceptions of public space in Africa. Cyprian Fisiy and Peter Geschiere (1996) point out that witchcraft historically has held a powerful role in political discourse, focusing on power, inequality, and tension between an individual's ambitions and communitarian values. However, in the early twenty-first century, in Africa's new urban centers and in its politics, press, sports, health care, educational institutions, and popular culture, the criteria for evaluating behavior in terms of the individual vis-à-vis the community is tied to broader societal issues of personal ambition and the growing inequalities in African society (Chabal and Daloz 1999, 63-76; Zeleza and Kalipeni 1999).

Patrick Chabal and Jean-Pascal Daloz (1999) take mainstream analysis to task for failing to understand that many of the concepts used to analyze Africa—democracy, multi-party elections, and political culture—have in practice been Africanized. Rather than concluding that Africa can't or won't modernize, Chabal and Daloz demonstrate that Africa works in a way that is different from Western societies, and the role of the state and the relationship between state and society is different. For these authors, there is a built-in bias for greater levels of disorder, and against the formation of Western-style legal, administrative, and institutional structures necessary for development (as we in and of the West define it). One of the keys to better understanding Africa is to realize that in the present time, cultural dynamics should be examined within the context of modern instrumental uses; that is, Africa's present circumstances encourage the creative use of "the traditional" (147). Chabal and Daloz make a powerful case for changing our paradigm for analyzing African politics (Chabal 1996).

Indeed, things are so different in Africa that Jean-Francoise Bayart, Stephen Ellis, and Beatrice Hibou's *The Criminalization of the State in Africa* suggests that it is returning to the "heart of darkness." The authors are careful to note that this is not a return to tradition or primitiveness, but rather the way in which Africa was first brought into the global economy and the international political system: through economies of extraction or predation, with foreigners leading the way, and with African partners using armed force assisting. In using this lens to analyze the current changes that are occurring in sub-Saharan Africa, the authors confront the politics, cultural myths, and economic practices that make Africa what it is today. They also use this framework to make suggestions to international aid donors regarding the consequences of giving aid.

African Public Administration in Transition

Contemporary southern Africa is rapidly changing terrain. Many have lamented the absence of political and leadership skills that have plagued the African nations that became independent after World War II. One result has been that African public bureaucracies, although constrained by policy decisions made by political leaders, have played a central role in the performance of leadership functions in development (Esman 1974; Vengroff, Belhaj and Ndiaye 1991).

In his comparison of African nations, for example, Ferrel Heady (1991) noted five commonalities about the nature of political leadership that in effect, suggest that knowledge of political processes in the developing countries is understandably still fragmentary and tentative. According to Heady, the absence of strong political leadership in these countries has resulted in political regimes that can be characterized by:

- Widely shared developmental ideologies as the source of basic political goals

- High reliance on the political sector for achieving results in society

- Widespread incipient or actual political stability

- "Modernizing" elitist leadership accompanied by a wide "political gap" between the rulers and the ruled

- Imbalances in political institutions, with the public bureaucracy often playing a more dominant role than other institutions

This has had profound effects on administrative management in the public sector. Moses Kiggundu, among others, has alluded to the organizational face of the "soft state": society pervades public organizations that are not "mature" enough, in the Weberian sense, to prevent this occurrence (1989, 44). James Nti (1989) has suggested that the political economic crisis has resulted in the further penetration of society into the state, with societal conditions replicated within the state's administrative organizations. In addition, Nti (1989, 124) identified some of these conditions: "shortages in pencils, duplicating papers, functioning typewriters, and photocopiers are rampant in many ministries and departments in a number of African countries." Together, these factors account for the description of the African state as "a commons susceptible to tragedy" (see Leonard 1991, 279-81).

At the same time, Louise G. White (1990, 36) noted that even recent reports by international development organizations such as the World Bank have recognized the need for "joint diagnostic exercise(s)...with a mix of technical, organizational and political analysis, and with due attention to organizational processes." Richard Vengroff, Mohammed Belhaj, and Momar Ndiaye (1991) suggest that although certain roles and characteristics are common to public managers in different African countries, contextual differences occurring on a country-by-country basis undermine generic management education and development efforts. These important observations are in stark contrast to earlier models of development which suggested that tropical Africa has been modernized from "without" rather than from "within" (Kautsky 1972, 162-63). The attendant need for greater flexibility, communication, adaptability and innovation in governmental as well as private and not-for-profit sector institutions, has placed additional burdens on African political regimes (Esman 1991, 153; Picard, Liviga and Garrity 1994, 124-26).

After reviewing the transferability of management education and development from the West to Africa, however, Merrick Jones suggested that African managers require somewhat different skills than do Western managers. Jones (1989, 84-85) suggests that more highly developed political and diplomatic skills are needed by Malawian managers in monitoring events that may affect them in relation to their bosses, other superiors, colleagues, subordinates, as well as demands from outside the agency, such as family or kinship groups. To this we can add Dennis Rondinelli's (1983) caveat: the imposition of modern management techniques (for example, participatory management) cannot be implemented successfully without first preparing the participants, those in government and out, who will be assuming new or different responsibilities. All of this suggests that greater flexibility, communication, adaptability, and innovation in public administration education and training may not be enough. Institution building may be needed as well to illuminate the path of greatest tractability and efficacy (Balogun 1989; Picard, Liviga, and Garrity 1994b). The implications of this have been nicely captured by N. Ronan (1993), who has advocated shifting away from competency-based approaches and toward seeking the greatest return on management education investment. This would link internal organizational efficiency to external effectiveness. We argue, however, that making this linkage is problematic without a reorientation in comparative public administration that takes the local context into effect.

The Need for Interpretive Approaches

Our reading of the literature points to the need for incorporating culture more centrally in the study of comparative public administration. In the case of the nations in sub-Saharan Africa, this presents a twofold challenge of conceptualization: understanding African culture, and using this understanding to inform interpretation.

What is culture and how does it impact public administration? While the standard definition of culture is that it is a pattern of behavior specific to a period or a people, unfortunately, as an analytical concept, culture is not easily operationalized. In large part, this is because culture is a dynamic concept. Political scientists, for example, tend to discuss political culture as a paradigm, yet the ongoing conflict and contestation of "the political" means that culture is often the product of a struggle (Chabal and Daloz 1999). Indeed, Deborah Durham (1999, 212) reminds us that just because a society has a common political culture does not mean that it is "intransigent, homogeneous, and consistent." How people experience culture, even their own culture, is not always clear.

African culture is even more problematic. Daniel Etounga-Manguelle, for example, notes that while African culture is not easily grasped, there is a foundation of shared values, attitudes, and institutions that provide a common base for understanding (2000, 67). He suggests that nine characteristics capture the subtleties and nuances of the "invisible forces" (77) influencing African societies in general, and organizational behavior in particular. These are:

- Hierarchical differences- These are substantial in African nations, causing superiors to be seen as "having the right to privilege" (68)

- Control over uncertainty- African societies are only able to exert such control through religion, which leads to the idea that nature is the master of man and the practice of immersing one's self in the moment (68-69)

- The tyranny of time- African societies are "anchored in the ancestral past" and do not have a "dynamic perception of the future," making policy planning difficult to achieve (69)

- Indivisible power and authority- Religion continues to play an important role in African affairs with leaders often linking religion to political power, claiming "magical powers" to dominate and leaving others to either use power to change leaders, or to maintain the status quo (70)

- The community dominates the individual- "African thought rejects any view of the individual as an autonomous and responsible person." In African public sector organizations the only person able to solve problems is the minister himself and "supervisors, managers, and other officials are there only for show" (71)

- Excessive conviviality and rejection of open conflict- Everything is a pretext for a celebration and there is an "inexhaustible need for communication" that emphasizes "personal warmth over content." This results in bureaucratic inefficiencies as petitioners seek to meet directly with the person in charge since this "eliminates the coldness of writing letters back and forth" (72)

- Inefficient homo economicus- "Value is measured by the 'is' and not the 'has'" resulting in poor economic management at all levels (73)

- The high costs of irrationalism- "Witchcraft is...an instrument of social coercion and a convenient political instrument to eliminate opposition," which breeds "inefficiency... corruption, and disrespect to basic human rights" (73-74)

- Cannibalistic and totalitarian societies- Africans "appear to destroy with their own hands what they have built" (75)

Taken together, these nine characteristics illustrate how management education and training programs designed in the West for Western managers will fall far short of making their mark in the context of African administration. Any analysis of African administrative performance will yield puzzling findings that do not seem to conform to administrative and managerial realities as we in the West define these.

This leads to the second challenge: to give culture a more central place in the analysis of African administrative systems in order to understand the complex phenomena of the socioeconomic, political and administrative contexts. How can this be done? We argue that the critical facet of interpretive approaches is a focus on administrative processes and how these processes link public organizations to particular societies. Of course, this means more than knowing about a host nation's culture and having an open mind about "the other." These are both necessary conditions. Administrative effectiveness ultimately is rooted in the dominant values of the local culture. Multiple models and practices within the cultural context of specific nations are required, however. In the discipline of policy analysis for example, the issue of "factual knowledge" has been critically addressed and this has resulted in a lively debate and the conclusion that facts and values are culturally conditioned. This important insight should inform comparative public administrative research. In the discipline of organizational analysis, the uses of language, rituals, and group norms have provided a different take on the importance of formal rules and procedures relative to images of organizations. This knowledge is also useful to the comparative study of public administration. Just what does constitute the forms and goals of administrative practice? Interpretive approaches suggest that the answer is situational, dependent upon the cultural context of the specific nation in question (Burrell and Morgan 1979; Conrad 1983; Joseph 1998; Morgan 1986; Putnam 1983).

Profiles of the Nations of Southern Africa

The politics of development in the southern Africa region have been colored by the Republic of South Africa's regional economic and military strength, in addition to the economic and political linkages of the neighboring countries to South Africa (most, like Mozambique, derive from colonial times). In the years preceding the end of apartheid, the Republic of South Africa's neighbors developed several regional associations (such as the Preferential Trade Area of Eastern and Southern Africa and Southern African Development Community) to pool economic resources, to develop their political strength and regional infrastructure, and to combat the continued domination of the region by South Africa (Thompson 1986; Msabaha and Shaw 1987). As Leonard Thompson has noted (1986, 264), the colonial wars in this region were among the last, and the new nations neighboring South Africa have been somewhat slower to start down the road to independence than the rest of the continent.

All of the southern African nations except Angola and Mozambique (formerly Portuguese colonies) were British colonies or were within the sphere of influence of the Republic of South Africa. By the mid-1980s all except Zimbabwe had more than a decade of independence and population growth rates across the other southern nations have been similar. The economies of these nations appear considerably different, with Zimbabwe, Tanzania, and Zambia having the largest GNPs and Botswana and Malawi the smallest. The microeconomies of Lesotho and Swaziland are somewhat separate cases (Young 1982, 191).

The average GNP per capita (again, excluding Lesotho and Swaziland for the moment) provides another perspective on the national political economies, with Botswana and Zimbabwe showing relatively higher income levels and Mozambique, Malawi, and Tanzania showing relatively lower levels. However, it is important to bracket this information because all of these nations are relatively poor (compare World Bank 1986 and 1999) and the estimates for per capita GNP reflected a downward trend beginning in the last decades of the twentieth century in most of the nations in sub-Saharan Africa (Nyang'oro 1989).

The remainder of this section provides a brief overview of the Southern African Development Community (SADC) countries. First, in tabular form, the basic demographic and economic data are presented, followed by a chart that shows the nature of the political cal systems in these nations. Then, brief narrative profiles of each SADC nation are given, and a listing of SADC websites completes the section.

Table 1: Selected Socioeconomic Data on SADC Countries

Country	Income Class	Population size (in millions)	Life Expectancy (years)	Infant Mortality (rate per 1000)	Literacy Rate	Caloric Intake (%)	*GNP per capita ($)
Angola	Lower Middle Income	13.1	46.7	154	**	**	$740
Botswana	Middle Income	1.70	38.1	80	78.9	93	$3430
Lesotho	Lower Middle Income	1.80	37.9	91	81.4	104	$590
Malawi	Low Income	10.70	37.5	113	61.8	95	$170
Mozambique	Low Income	18.4	41.1	128	46.5	**	$210
South Africa	Middle Income	45.3	46.5	52	86.0	**	$2780
Swaziland	Lower Middle Income	1.1	43.7	106	80.9	80	$1350
Tanzania	Low Income	35.2	43.1	104	77	98	$290
Zambia	Lower Middle Income	10.2	36.9	102	79.9	84	$380
Zimbabwe	Lower Middle Income	13.0	39.0	76	90	82	$480

Source: Information on the above are drawn from the World Bank Group. World Development Indicators Database, April 2004
(HYPERLINK "http://www.worldbank.org/data/countrydata/countrydata.html"
http://www.worldbank.org/data/countrydata/countrydata.html).
*In 1980, the World Bank used monetary criteria, expressed in Gross National Product (GNP) per capita, to categorize the countries of the world. Those countries whose GNP per capita in 1978 was below U.S. $370 were referred to as low-income, and the lower-middle-income countries were those whose GNP per capita ranged from $370-$3500.
** Data are unavailable for these indicators.

Botswana

Botswana is a land-locked country in southern Africa; it was one of the forty-nine low income countries of the world and also one of the twenty-nine countries considered by the United Nations as the least developed in the world (Kurian 1987). Botswana became independent in 1966 when it was proclaimed a republic. Botswana has adopted a consistently moderate and rational policy toward race relations (Vengroff 1976). It has not given up any part of the British legacy that seemed to promote the country's constitutional, educational, and economic progress. Relations with the United Kingdom and South Africa are generally cordial. Furthermore, more than a decade after independence, British civil servants continued to hold many senior administrative positions (Hartland-Thurnberg 1978).

Botswana is a multiparty state and also has had one of the most stable governments in Africa. They have held fair and regular elections every five years since 1969 (Danevard 1995). The President is elected by the National Assembly for a five-year term. A bicameral Parliament consists of the House of Chiefs and the National Assembly. In Botswana, industrial activities are concentrated in the towns of Lobatse and Francistown, but are limited to processing livestock. According to George Kurian (1987), although foreign investment is encouraged, the most recent foreign investments have been in the mining sector.

Compulsory, universal free education is the eventual goal in Botswana, but its introduction was delayed for economic reasons. Higher education is provided by the Joint University of Botswana and Swaziland; however, some Bostwana citizens study abroad (Colclough and McCarthy 1980).

Botswana has continued to have a substantial non-African population, which plays an active political and economic role. The largest non-African groups are 1,400 Britons; 3,400 South Africans; 2,700 Zimbabweans; in addition to some Asians (Kurian 1987).

Botswana has maintained one of the world's highest growth rates since its independence in 1966. Through fiscal discipline and sound management, Botswana has transformed itself from one of the poorest countries in the world to a middle-income country with a per capita GDP of $6,600 in 2000. Diamond mining has fueled much of Botswana's economic expansion and currently accounts for more than one-third of GDP and for three-fourths of export earnings. Tourism, subsistence farming, and cattle-raising are other key sectors (CIA World Factbook 2000).

Lesotho

Lesotho is described as an enclave located within the east central part of South Africa; it is the only Anglophonic country in the world entirely surrounded by another. Until its independence in 1966, Lesotho was under British rule as a crown protectorate. British colonial policy toward Basutoland (Lesotho's name prior to independence) was characterized by parsimony and indifference. The actual governance was left to the numerous chieftains who opposed all attempts to centralize and modernize administration (Thompson 1975).

Under the terms of the constitution of 1965, which was suspended in 1970, Lesotho was a constitutional monarchy with a bicameral legislature. After a coup in 1986, legislative and executive powers were vested in the king but actually exercised by a six-member military council and a twenty-member council of ministers. In 1993 Lesotho adopted a new constitution that redefined the role of the monarchy and altered the legislative branch of the government. The king, who is the head of state, has no executive or legislative authority. The Prime Minister holds executive power. The prime minister is the leader of the majority party in the National Assembly and is responsible for appointing a cabinet. The legislative body includes the National Assembly, consisting of eighty members elected by universal adult suffrage, and a thirty-three-member Senate, made up of traditional chiefs and nominated representatives. Lesotho has ten districts subdivided into wards and administered by hereditary chiefs (CIA World Factbook 2000).

Lesotho is one of the low-income countries of the world, and one of the twenty-nine countries considered by the United Nations to be most seriously affected by adverse economic conditions (Bardhill and Cobbe 1985). Lesotho has a free market economy in which the dominant sector is private; it has few natural resources and its economy is based on export of labor and tourism receipts. The main sources of foreign aid to Lesotho are the United Kingdom, the United States, Canada, Denmark, and Sweden (Kurian 1987). Apart from a few thousand Europeans and a few hundred Asians, the population of Lesotho is Basotho.

Malawi

Malawi is a landlocked country in southeastern Africa and is also a former British colony. Malawi is one of the forty-nine low-income countries and one of the twenty-nine countries classified as among the least developed in the world. It has a free market economy in which the dominant sector is private (Kurian 1987).

In Malawi the legal basis of government is the constitution of 1966, which established a one-party state, parliamentary form of government, and strong president. However, Malawi has been taking steps to make a transition to be pluralistic and open its political and economic systems. As Mekki Mtewa (1984) explains, Malawi's political processes do not permit the existence of organized dissent because of ingrained social values favoring hierarchical relationships, respect for authority, and a desire to work through consensus and avoid conflict. All civil servants are appointed (or dismissed) by the president although nominal control of the service is held by the Civil Service Commission. Recruits for top government positions are either trained at the Malawi Institute of Public Administration or sent abroad for training and education in the United States, the United Kingdom, Canada, India, or West Germany (Kurian 1987).

The manufacturing and industrial sectors in Malawi are dominated by foreign capital. Private foreign investors are attracted to Malawi because of its political stability and the incentives offered. Industrial sites are offered at low cost; market studies and feasibility surveys are financed by the government; exclusive production licenses are granted for a specified period; and adequate guarantees are provided against nationalizing industry. The most effective inducements are liberal provisions for the repatriations of profit and capital, traffic protection, and generous depreciation allowances.

Malawi's economy is predominately agricultural, with about 90% of the population living in rural areas. Agriculture accounts for 37% of GDP and 85% of export revenues. The economy depends on substantial inflows of economic assistance from the IMF, the World Bank, and individual donor nations. In late 2000, Malawi was approved for relief under the Heavily Indebted Poor Countries (HIPC) program. The government faces strong challenges, for example, to fully develop a market economy, to improve educational facilities, to face up to environmental problems, and to deal with the rapidly growing problem of HIV/AIDS (CIA World Factbook 2000).

In Malawi, Africans constitute 95.5% of the population. British and Asian persons constitute the remainder (Kurian 1987).

South Africa

South Africa, the southernmost country in Africa, is bordered on the north by Namibia, Botswana, Zimbabwe, Mozambique, and Swaziland; on the east and south by the Indian Ocean; and on the west by the Atlantic Ocean. Lesotho forms an enclave in the northeastern part of the country. South Africa has a diverse and dramatic landscape. Most of the interior is covered by high plateaus, which are separated from the country's long coastline by chains of tall mountains. South Africa is rich in minerals such as gold and diamonds, and its industrial base grew up around the mining industry.

After the British seized the Cape of Good Hope area in 1806, many of the Dutch settlers (the Boers) trekked north to found their own republics. The discovery of diamonds (1867) and gold (1886) spurred wealth and immigration and intensified the subjugation of the native inhabitants. The Boers resisted the British encroachments, but were eventually defeated in the Boer War (1899-1902). The resulting Union of South Africa operated under a policy of apartheid, the separate development of the races. The 1990s brought an end to political apartheid and ushered in black majority rule (CIA World Factbook 2003).

South Africa gained its independence from the United Kingdom on 31 May 1910. However, it became a republic in 1961 following an October 1960 referendum. The post-apartheid constitution was certified by the Constitutional Court on 4 December 1996, and entered into effect on 3 February 1997, to be implemented in phases. South Africa's legal system is based on Roman-Dutch law and English common law.

Parliament is the legislative authority of South Africa and has the power to make laws for the country in accordance with the Constitution. It consists of the National Assembly and the National Council of Provinces (NCOP). Parliamentary sittings are open to the public. Since the establishment of the Parliament in 1994, a number of steps have been taken to make it more accessible. This has been done to make the institution more accountable, as well as to motivate and facilitate public participation in the legislative process. One of these steps is the establishment of the website, which encourages comments and feedback from the public (Burger 2002).

South Africa is a middle-income, emerging market with an abundant supply of natural resources. It has well-developed financial, legal, communication, energy, and transport sectors, with a stock exchange that ranks among the ten largest in the world. It boasts a modern infrastructure supporting an efficient distribution of goods to major urban centers throughout the region. However, growth has not been strong enough to lower South Africa's high unemployment rate, and daunting economic problems (poverty and a lack of economic empowerment among the disadvantaged) remain from the apartheid era. High crimes and HIV/AIDS infection rates also deter investment. South African economic policy is fiscally conservative but pragmatic, focusing on targeting inflation and liberalizing trade as a means of increasing job growth and household income (CIA World Factbook 2003).

Black Africans comprise three quarters of South Africa's population, and whites, Coloreds (people of mixed race), and Asians (mainly Indians) make up the remainder. Among the black population there are numerous ethnic groups and eleven official languages. Until recently, whites dominated the non-white majority population under the political system of racial segregation known as apartheid. Apartheid ended in the early 1990s, but South Africa is still recovering from the racial inequalities in political power, opportunity, and lifestyle. The end of apartheid led to the lifting of trade sanctions against South Africa imposed by the international community. It also led to a total reorganization of the government based on majority rule.

South Africa is divided into nine provinces: Gauteng, Northern Province, Mpumalanga, North-West Province, Free State, Eastern Cape, Northern Cape, Western Cape, and KwaZulu-Natal. The country has three capitals: Cape Town is the legislative capital; Pretoria, the executive capital; and Bloemfontein, the judicial capital (http://encarta.msn.com).

South Africa took a census in October 1996 that showed a population of 40,583,611 (after an official adjustment for a 6-8% under enumeration based on a post enumeration survey). Estimates for this country explicitly take into account the effects of excess mortality due to AIDS. This, according to the report, results in lower life expectancy, higher infant morality and death rates, lower population and growth rates, and changes in the distribution of population by age and sex than might otherwise be expected.

A breakdown of ethnic groups shows the following: blacks 75.2%; whites 13.6%; Colored 8.6%; Indian 2.6%. Literacy rates for the total population of ages fifteen and over who can read and write is 86.4% (male 87%; female 85.7%). Some of the key industrial activities in South Africa include mining, automobile assembly, metalworking, machinery, textile, iron and steel, chemicals, foodstuffs (CIA World Factbook 2003). South Africa is the world's largest producer of platinum, gold and chromium.

Swaziland

Landlocked Swaziland is located in southern Africa. It shares its international boundary with two neighbors: South Africa and Mozambique. Swaziland, a former British colony, is one of the thirty-nine lower-middle income countries of the world with a free market economy dominated by the private sector (Potholm 1972).

Swaziland is a constitutional monarchy without a constitution. The king exercises tremendous influence. While political power is not confined to the royal family, it is concentrated there. The system of government is said to provide for extensive consultation and depends on consensus building. The people are encouraged to bring their views to the local chiefs in private or in public meetings. The formulation of opposition parties is discouraged (Booth 1983; Kurian 1987).

For a small underdeveloped country, Swaziland has a relatively well-developed manufacturing sector contributing 23% of the gross domestic product and employing 12.3% of the workforce. Originally limited to processing of agricultural produce, Swaziland has diversified into wood pulp, cement, confectionary, brewing, textiles, agricultural machinery, fertilizers, and color television assembly.

Higher education is provided by the Joint University of Botswana and Swaziland and by institutions in the United States, the United Kingdom, and Canada. The population of Swaziland is more homogeneous than that of other countries in sub-Saharan Africa. Of the African population, which makes up 96% of the total population, over half is Swazi while the other half belongs to the Zulu, Tonga, and Shangaan tribes. Ethnic minorities include 10,695 Europeans (Afrikaaners, Britons, and Portuguese) (Kurian, 1987).

Tanzania

Tanzania is located in East Africa, south of the Equator. As a former British colony, it shares its international boundaries with eight countries: Uganda, Kenya, Mozambique, Malawi, Zambia, Zaire, Burundi, and Rwanda. Tanzania became independent in 1961. It is one of the forty-nine low-income countries of the world; it is also one of the twenty-nine countries considered by the United Nations to be among the least developed; and also one of the forty-five countries considered to be most seriously affected by adverse economic conditions. Tanzania has a free market economy in which the dominant sector is public (Kurtz 1978; Kim 1980).

Tanzania was a one-party dominant, modified democracy from 1961 until the early 1980s. Its constitution was amended in 1992 to end the constitutional supremacy of the governing party. Tanzania held its first-ever multi-party presidential election in October 1995 (USAID Congressional Presentation FY 1997). Tanzania is one of the most stable nations in Africa, having had only two presidents since independence and having suffered no internal turmoil or external invasion. Despite one of the most heterogeneous populations in the world, there are no separatist movements. The ruling party, Chama Cha Mapinduzi (CCM), formerly the Tanganyikan African Union (TANU), has dominated politics so completely that there is little room for an opposition movement to thrive.

The Civil Service is regulated by the Civil Service Commission, which conducts examinations, determines salary scales, and regulates promotion. The Central Recruiting Section of the Commission recruits from within the country but also from abroad, and many technical and professional positions are filled through external recruitment. Training programs for civil servants are conducted at the Civil Service Training Center and the Institute of Public Administration (Kurian 1987).

Tanzania is one of the poorest countries in the world. The economy is heavily dependent on agriculture, which accounts for half of GDP, provides 85% of exports, and employs 80% of the workforce. Topography and climatic conditions, however, limit cultivated crops to only 4% of the land area. Industry is mainly limited to processing agricultural products and light consumer goods. The World Bank, the IMF, and bilateral donors have provided funds to rehabilitate Tanzania's deteriorated economic infrastructure. Growth in 1991-2000 showed an upswing in industrial production and a substantial increase in output of minerals led by gold. Natural gas exploration in the Rufiji Delta looks promising and production could start by 2002. Recent banking reforms have helped increase private sector growth and investment. With continued donor support and solid macroeconomic policies, Tanzania's real GDP growth rate was forecast to be 6% in 2001 and 2002 (CIA World Factbook 2000).

In Tanzania it is often difficult to distinguish between the public and private sectors because the National Development Corporation participates in industrial promotion even in the private sector. Ownership of the private sector is almost entirely in the hands of Europeans and Asians. Lack of experience, financing and technical expertise has inhibited the emergence of an African entrepreneurial class in Tanzania. Most of the private foreign capital is invested in plantations (Coulson 1982). Higher education in Tanzania is provided at the University College in Dar es Salaam, and other students are enrolled in higher learning institutions in countries such as the United States, the United Kingdom, Canada, India, West Germany, Hungary and at the Vatican. Africans form 90% of the country's population. The remainder are Asians and Europeans (Darch 1985).

Zambia

Zambia is a landlocked country located in southern Africa between the Zambezi River and the southern rim of the Congo Basin. It shares its international boundaries with eight countries: Mozambique, Zimbabwe, Botswana, South West Africa, Angola, Zaire, Tanzania, and Malawi. Zambia gained its independence in 1964 and is one of the thirty-nine lower-middle income countries of the world with a free market economy in which the dominant sector is public (Williams 1984).

The government in Zambia is a one-party participating democracy with a strong presidency. The political system is open to individuals' divergent opinions, provided they are willing to work within the one-party structure and not challenge the president's preeminent position (Tordoff 1975; Gertzel 1984). Zambia has had what can be described as a mixed economy despite substantial governmental participation in the industrial and marketing sectors through the parastatal system. Although foreign investments are encouraged in Zambia, they have been progressively reduced through nationalization. These foreign investments are also encouraged through a liberal policy permitting unlimited remittances of profits abroad (Daniel 1979).

Despite progress in privatization and budget reform, Zambia's economy has a long way to go. Privatization of government-owned copper mines relieved the government from covering mammoth losses generated by the industry and greatly improved the chances for copper mining to return to profitability and spur economic growth. In late 2000, Zambia was determined to be eligible for debt relief under the Heavily Indebted Poor Countries (HIPC) initiative. Inflation and unemployment rates remain high, but the GDP growth rate was expected to rise in 2001 (CIA World Factbook 2000).

Higher education is provided by the University of Zambia, and some Zambian students are also enrolled in institutions of higher learning abroad in the United States, the United Kingdom, India, Canada, and Australia. Nearly 99% of Zambians are Africans belonging to more than seventy Bantu-speaking tribes. There are three major ethnic minorities: Asians, Coloreds and Europeans (Kurian 1987).

Zimbabwe

Zimbabwe is located in south central Africa between the Zambezi River on the north and the Limpopo River on the south. Its international border is shared with four neighbors: Mozambique, South

Africa, Botswana, and Zambia. Zimbabwe gained its independence in 1980 and is one of the thirty-nine lower-middle income countries of the world with a free market economy in which the private sector is dominant (Weinrich 1978).

The Zimbabwe government is a parliamentary democracy; it is a sovereign republic with a president as head of state and a prime minister elected by the House of Assembly as head of government. Zimbabwe has a multiparty political system. The largest parties are the ruling Zimbabwe African National Union (ZAPU) and the Patriotic Front. There are a number of minor political parties, none of which are

---

Box 1
Websites of the SADC Member Countries

Country	Internet Address
Botswana	www.gov.bw www.sadc.int/english/countries/botswana.htm
Lesotho	www.sadc.int/english/countries/lesotho.htm
Malawi	www.sadc.int/english/countries/malawi.htm
Mozambique	www.sadc.int/english/countries/mozambique.htm
Namibia	http://www.sadc.int/english/countries/namibia.htm www.sadc.int/english/countries/namibia.htm
South Africa	http://www.cia.gov/cia/publications/factbook/geos/ www.cia.gov/cia/publications/factbook/geos/Sf.html
Swaziland	www.swazi.com/government/ www.sadc.int/english/countries/swaziland.htm
Tanzania	www.sadc.int/english/countries/tanzania.htm
Zambia	www.sadc.int/english/countries.zambia.htm
Zimbabwe	www.sadc.int/english/countries.zimbabwe.htm
Angola	www.angola.org www.sadc.int/english/countries/angola.htm
SADC Organization	www.nsrc.org www.sadc.int/

---

represented in the House of Assembly. There are over 24,000 civil servants in Zimbabwe. The Public Service Board controls the administration and discipline of the civil service (Kurian 1987).

The government of Zimbabwe faces a variety of difficult economic problems as it struggles to consolidate earlier moves to develop a market-oriented economy. Its involvement in the war in the Democratic Republic of Congo, for example, has already drained hundreds of millions of dollars from the economy. Badly needed support from the IMF suffered delays in part because of the country's failure to meet budgetary goals. Inflation rose from an annual rate of 32% in 1998 to 59% in 1999 and 60% in 2000.

The economy is being steadily weakened by excessive government deficits and AIDS because Zimbabwe has the highest rate of infection in the world. Per capita GDP, which is twice the average of the poorest sub-Saharan nations, will increase little if any in the near future, and Zimbabwe will suffer continued frustrations in developing its agricultural and mineral resources (CIA World Factbook 2000).

Despite growing diversification in industry, food processing remains the single, largest branch of manufacturing and the largest employer of the nation's labor force. Higher education is provided at the University College of Zimbabwe. Zimbabwean students are also enrolled in institutions of higher learning abroad in the United States, the United Kingdom, Australia, and Canada. Ethnically, Zimbabwe is composed of four distinct groups: black Africans, whites (called Europeans, irrespective of national origin), Asians (mainly East Indians) and Coloreds. Blacks constitute 96% of the population, whites 3.55%, and Indians and Coloreds 0.5% (Schatzberg 1984; Kumbula 1979).

The Organization of the Book

This first chapter has established the broad contours of our arguments describing the basic influences in sub-Saharan Africa, and identifying some of the more critical voices and their contributions to developing a more culturally sensitive understanding of African politics and administration. We also briefly introduced the specific nations that serve as the empirical focus of our analysis.

In the next two chapters, we argue that the absence of a culturally sensitive orientation in the macro-oriented models used for the study of comparative and development public administration has impeded the analysis of development in southern Africa. We suggest that the positivistic and orthodox orientations of elements of these models take for granted certain characteristics that are all too often missing in the states of southern Africa. Furthermore, these approaches are incapable of capturing the varieties of meanings embedded in administrative activities and practices within the ranks of developing nations that are characterized by constant change and ongoing transformations as we enter the twenty-first century.

Chapter 4 addresses how comparative public administration research can utilize culture as a variable in assessing African bureaucracy. It focuses specifically on the nine original members of the Southern African Development Community (SADC). The chapter begins the process of reframing (Bolman and Deal 1991) the challenges of public administration and goes on to establish the interpretive basis for understanding the characteristics of administration in a new light. The rest of the chapter is then devoted to an in-depth discussion of the cultural realities of conducting public administration in Africa in general, and in the Southern African countries in particular. Based on the cultural perspectives and arguments presented, the chapter offers a more useful culture-based framework for grappling with the dynamics of administration in these African countries. The chapter closes on a prospective note with a discussion of the relationship between a cultural focus of administration and important issues of globalization, economic development, democratization, and governance.

Chapter 5 explores the relationships that exist between a culturally sensitive view of public administration and important dimensions of public administration and management. In our case, we focus on managing inter-organizational relations, managing intra-organizational relations, managing community relations, and strategies that are needed for managing "intensive" growth in developing and emerging societies. This treatment is consistent with other studies, (Sorenson 1991) which have noted the shift from extensive to intensive growth; that is, a reframing away from an emphasis on the global economy toward the domestic and regional economies. This shift requires paying closer attention to culture in evolving new capacities to formulate and implement growth policies, including greater flexibility, communication, adaptability and innovation in all sectors of society. The chapter ends with a discussion of how public administrators can fruitfully participate in the process of fostering a culturally based mode for administrative practice.

In a world where nothing is solid and everything is changing, it is tempting to follow familiar paths and to use the same old solutions regardless of how much the problems have changed. Our sixth chapter provides an explicit link between the adoption of a culturally-sensitive focus for viewing public organizations and a more in-depth understanding of the dynamics of public administration in southern African organizations. The chapter also shows how developing countries can take advantage of a culturally based approach to enhance other dimensions of development such as globalization, economic development, democratization, and decentralization. The chapter concludes with a brief discussion of the relevancy of this approach for an ongoing assessment of development public administration.

In a brief epilogue we discuss the role of culture in understanding post-apartheid South Africa, examining five areas critical to nation-building: the new structure of government, the role of change agents in the immediate transition period, the African National Congress's Reconstruction and Development Program, the Ncholo Report on the public service, and the 2004 Cape Town Olympic Games bid. While the road ahead looks difficult in South Africa, understanding how culture influences choices can provide a framework for addressing the challenges of the post-apartheid transformation.

Chapter Two

Characteristics of Administration in Developing Nations

"Administration" is a generic term that lends itself to various interpretations. Virtually everywhere one looks in both developed and developing nations, bureaucratic organizations extensively influence political, social and economic life. It is widely assumed that the structural characteristics of organizations properly defined as "bureaucratic" (Weber 1958) influence the behavior of individuals, whether clients or bureaucrats, who interact with them (Hummel 1986).

This chapter provides an overview of the basic concepts from the comparative and development public administration literature. First, at a theoretical level, we discuss the term "administration." Second, we explore the key dimensions of administration that emerge from the theoretical conceptualizations. Third, we discuss some of the deficiencies or limits of the past comparative public administration orientation. In particular, we identify and highlight any useful criticisms that may exist in the literature concerning the context of bureaucracy and its relationship to policy making and the differences existing between administrative processes and outcomes. Our review is necessarily brief, and our focus quickly moves to the literature on sub-Saharan Africa.

Past Uses of the Term "Administration"

A 1975 report to the US Office of Management and Budget by the Interagency Study Committee on Policy Management

Assistance identified three core elements of administration in the public sector:

- Policy management: the identification of needs, analysis of options, selection of programs, and allocation of resources on a jurisdiction-wide basis

- Resource management: the establishment of basic administrative support systems, such as budgeting, financial management, procurement and supply, and personnel management

- Program management: the implementation of policy or daily operation of agencies carrying out policy along functional lines (Mushkin, Sandifer, and Familton 1978, 10)

These characteristics of administration comprise the activities involved in carrying out the policies and programs of government. For example, John Gaus (1940) includes as "administration" the problems, powers, organization, and methods of management employed in enforcing the law and in discharging governmental responsibilities. Administration is also used in a broader sense to include some responsibility, varying widely in degree among governments and departments, in determining what the policies and programs of government should be, as well as how these should be executed. According to this view, characteristics of administration focus principally on the planning, organizing, directing, coordinating, and controlling of government operations (Mosher 1982; Gulick and Urwick 1937). Such universal sub-processes of administration, according to Robert Pursley and Norman Snortland (1980, 12), are both interrelated and independent and are usually, but not necessarily, carried out simultaneously and continuously in an ongoing enterprise.

In a recent study of nine African countries, John Montgomery (1986B) looked at the characteristics of administration based on the functions performed. His analysis drew heavily on Henry Mintzberg's (1979) contention that top public administrators occupy what is sometimes called the "strategic apex" of the managerial system in their countries. These functions fell into three distinct categories: supervising the work of the organization, handling its relationship with the environment, and developing its strategy for change in response to external forces. Managers with "supervisory" responsibilities, therefore, would be expected to (1) allocate resources, (2) handle disturbances, (3) monitor performance, (4) disseminate information, and (5) provide leadership in staffing and motivating employees. In "managing the environment," they would (6) serve as spokesperson for the organization's activities, (7) provide liaison with other organizations,

(8) negotiate with members of other organizations, and (9) act as figureheads in carrying out ceremonial or representational duties on behalf of the organization. Finally, in developing the organization's strategy for "responding to that environment," they would (10) act as entrepreneurs in adapting its mission and devising means of achieving its major goals.

While Henry Mintzberg's categories are comprehensive, others have addressed the issue. Shmuel Noah Eisenstadt (1964) suggests three normative bureaucratic orientations: service to others, passive tool, and self-aggrandizement. These represent a structural functional view of administrative behavior. Milton Esman (1966) proposed two provocative poles of administrative behavior—the creative entrepreneur and the controlled instrument—reflecting the normative characteristics of administration. Edward Weidner (1970) suggested six major bureaucratic roles (innovator, leader, change agent, administrator of processes routine, specialists or technical expert, and political or administrative liaison) that present a mixture of various administrative characteristics.

In terms of African administration, John Montgomery (1987) proposed that one characteristic of administrators is that they should be engaged in activities that are instrumental to ultimate national purposes. According to this view, these are easily recognizable instrumental goals that facilitate the grand developmental purposes promoted by politicians and statesmen and make up much of managerial activity. As such, administration consists of:

1. Influencing development strategies or emphases of specific investment decisions

2. Introducing a new agricultural, industrial, or commercial enterprise in the country

3. Developing a local capacity for an activity formerly dependent on external resources

4. Discovering a solution or a more promising approach to a significant problem

5. Stimulating the more widespread adoption of a preferred practice or other desired public response

6. Introducing a new service or program

7. Raising standards of products or services provided

8. Changing rules or procedures to be more responsive to the needs of clients

9. Avoiding disruption of services by timely action despite difficulties or risks

10. Securing a national advantage or resource by negotiations

11. Improving or expanding dissemination of programs or techniques

12. Developing more effective working relationships with local agencies or sources of external aid

13. Introducing or expanding the use of analytic, data-based management aids

15. Introducing cost or time-saving measures and ideas

16. Imposing tighter structure or controls on staff or vendor performance

17. Improving the allocation or organization of responsibilities and functions

18. Upgrading the caliber, capabilities, or morale of staff

19. Upgrading physical facilities or equipment

20. Improving record keeping or information retrieval systems (American Institutes for Research 1974)

A major investigation of the skills needed in southern African nations was undertaken in the early 1980s (NASPAA 1984). Of the forty-six skills studied, the seven most important were: technical skills, writing skills, knowledge of procedures, financial management, negotiation skills, supervision, and bureaucratic politics. The ten least frequently encountered general skills were: impact analysis, contingency management, inter-organizational skills, language skills, disaster management, program analysis, inventory management, computational skills, economic analysis, and community relations.

This brief overview shows that administration is comprised of not only those activities administrators perform, but also those functions that are instrumental to ultimate national purposes. This linkage is especially important for development administration and serves to draw the boundaries within which public administrators and managers function. However, since not all skills are utilized equally, we next need to examine certain primary skills that administrators ought to possess.

Some Key Characteristics of Administration

John Gaus (1936) suggested that in order for administrative officials to fulfill the goals for which they are called upon to serve, such as organizing economic programs, planning for conservation of natural resources, coordinating human and material resources, and motivating subordinates, they must have the tools of administration at their disposal. Richard Vengroff and Alan Johnston (1984; 1985) carried out a study of decentralization in the implementation of rural development programs, and included the training needs of mid-level development agents in the Senegalese bureaucracy. Findings from these studies suggested that the lack of success in administration was a function of the set of skill-related characteristics that administrative officials exhibited.

Howard McCurdy compiled a list of the most frequently exported management strategies needed to help developing nations. Some of these strategies were: modern management techniques including organization management techniques; technical skill development; planning; financial and budgetary management; and institution building, which includes the art of bureaucratic politics (McCurdy 1977, 305).

After extensive research efforts on development management in Africa, Philip Morgan came up with some of the same kinds of skills identified by other scholars. According to Morgan, "managerial qualities crucial to effective implementation of centrally inspired policy includes skills in negotiation, representation, coordination, motivation, advocacy, work planning and allocation, monitoring, reporting, and so on" (1984, 5). And in a recent study using management events data gathered from southern Africa, Ogwo Umeh (1990) identified six key dimensions of administration that are believed to commonly influence the conduct of public administration in the seven southern African countries that were the focus of his study. What these and other studies show is that the skills needed by administrators are many. The remainder of this section discusses the six skill "clusters" that encompass the demands most commonly placed on administrators in developing countries.

A. Technical Skills

This skill category represents the specialized knowledge required to effectively perform organizational missions. It incorporates the ability to perform various secretarial duties, mathematics, and computational techniques. Technical skills can also be defined in terms of having expertise or being able to accomplish a procedure in a systematic way.

J. Clifton Williams (1978, 76-78) associates technical skills with individuals having an unusually high tendency and ability to perform various developmental functions in a special manner. He contends that people with high technical skills are particularly influential and exhibit high competence when it comes to problem solving. The World Development Report (World Bank 1983) notes that although developing nations have made remarkable progress in education and training, most nations still have large reserves of unskilled labor alongside severe shortages of skilled people. Technical skills are of crucial importance in the developing countries because their presence could alleviate the problems involved in food production, health services provision, improvement of quality of life and overall societal development. Furthermore, if developing countries could commit more resources to enhancing their technical capabilities they could benefit by saving a good part of the technical assistance often used to finance foreigners to come in and provide these technical services. Although skill shortages are hard to quantify, the World Bank finds that two-thirds of its borrowing countries face serious difficulties filling certain posts requiring technical competence in the public sector. The evidence suggests that technical skills have an important role to play in administration.

From a development perspective, Coralie Bryant and Louise G. White suggest that technical skills are of particular importance because they are a central factor in the environment of people living through change (Bryant and White 1982, 87). Aside from being directly related to productivity, technical skills provide guidelines for defining jobs and for structuring an organization (Dresang 1984, 116).

Technical skills, and technology itself, are sometimes seen as provoking controversy in the administrative setting by challenging traditional professions. From lower to higher levels, people work with tools: the peasant with his or her hoe, the extension agent with a new seed variety, and the supervisor with computer-processed information. The acquisition of tractors frees landowners from sharecropping arrangements, so they feel more comfortable about this new technology than those who were put out of work by its introduction. Computers and computer skills allow managers to collect data about the productivity of field agents, so managers feel more positively about computers than agents (Bryant and White 1982, 88). Controversy aside, technical skills will clearly impact the performance and character of bureaucracies in developing countries.

B. General Management Skills

These management skills are described in terms of organizational members having the ability to manage, control, and organize resources. This category includes specific management functions such as planning, organizing, staffing, directing, personnel management, and budgeting.

Much of what an administrator does is "general management." He or she must secure staff, office space, coordinate people and activities, and purchase the supplies needed to complete assigned tasks. He or she must gather records and organize them in a way that provides timely access. The administrator must also conduct evaluations and analyses in order to identify strengths and weaknesses in projects and programs being performed. Administrators then need to remedy problems before they become unmanageable or fatal to the organization.

Perhaps the best expression of general management skills has been described by Luther Gulick and Lyndall Urwick (1937, 3-13) while speculating on the work of the chief executive. According to these scholars, a manager must have the ability to perform eight unique but related functions. These functions are planning, organizing, staffing, directing, coordinating, reporting and budgeting (known as POSDCORB). The importance of this conceptualization is that POSDCORB captures the organizing and managing functions of public administration.

Taken together, general management skills are those that enable an administrator to implement organizational activities. Traditionally, it has been assumed that the skills would be equally important across various administrative systems. It is often suggested that particularly in a developing country, general management skills are especially valuable because given the paucity of both human and material resources these skills enable officials to make up for limited resources (Landau 1969, 346-358).

Essentially general management skills do help managers bring together scarce resources. This is especially important when faced with "accomplishing" enormously complex, but horrendously ill-defined, objectives.

C. Analytic Management Skills

This category of skills is described in terms of the ability to critically examine and evaluate various aspects of a program or policy with a view to recommending needed action to the bureaucracy. Analytical management skills involve policy analysis, financial analysis, project/program analysis, impact analysis, data analysis, and evaluation/monitoring.

An analytic management skill is defined as the application of rigorous techniques of analysis to organizational management and policy implementation challenges. These skills become more needed as demands on government become more complex. Analytical management skills, including impact analysis, data analysis, economics, evaluation and monitoring, are highly specialized, require a substantial amount of training, and involve high levels of quantitative sophistication as well.

D. Organizational Flexibility Skills

Organizational flexibility is described in terms of the ability to respond and adapt to changing organizational contingencies. This cluster of skills involves flexibility in organizational management, motivation, management adaptation, leadership, and initiative.

Organizational flexibility as an administrative skill category is the ability of the organization and its leaders to adapt to a changing environment. It is an important capacity, particularly in the developing nations, since there is a high level of environmental turbulence that impacts the ability of organizations to function. In fact, one of the issues often addressed in the literature of development administration is the extent to which Third World organizations adopt a "learning" approach to administration (Korten 1980), and the extent to which they maintain some degree of flexibility to accommodate change in the environment.

Perhaps topmost in this cluster of activities is the ability of administrators to motivate subordinates to adapt to changing circumstances that may not be in their immediate best interests. One might question the need to emphasize this type of skill in Africa since organizations are usually created to perform very specific functions. According to Samuel Huntington (1965), when the organization confronts a changing environment survival dictates action, and the organization's commitment to its original function may weaken. The ability of the organization to deal with this type of situation depends very much on the presence of people who can cope with change. Other researchers also have found that rather than demand a heavy emphasis on strict adherence to formal work rules, greater discretion, flexibility and initiative are needed if development administration is to be successful (Montgomery 1980; Morgan 1979; Vengroff 1983).

E. Political Maneuvering Skills

This skill is defined in terms of organizational actors having the ability to be politically astute, particularly when it comes to struggling to protect their agencies from attack by other political actors. Political maneuvering involves specific activities that include the ability to negotiate, the ability to understand the political environment, the ability to understand bureaucratic politics, and the ability to handle inter-organizational relations.

Political maneuvering, a term often used interchangeably with bureaucratic politics, has been researched quite extensively (Bryant and White 1982; Montgomery 1986). Here, we define political maneuvering as the ability of organizational leaders to protect their agency and its budget/ programs from attack by others. What kinds of activities cluster under this type of skill category, or as Montgomery puts it, what do bureaucrats wrangle over? No one would be surprised, he notes, to discover that the issues are money, turf, other bureaucrats, and policy (Montgomery 1986).

Montgomery points out that most of what academicians know about bureaucratic politics comes from large-scale studies that tell us why big organizations make big mistakes. Past research has examined, for instance, why the American military was unable to take advantage of intelligence information that warned of an attack on Pearl Harbor; why missiles were not withdrawn from Turkey in accordance with a presidential order; why individual members of a bureaucratic organization were denied official recognition for their achievements; and more recently, why the space shuttle Challenger exploded in mid-air and why the terrorist attack of September 11, 2001, changed the world.

Such examples also exist in developing countries. Robert Seidman wrote extensively about the non-implementability of national planning efforts, not because the plans were not drawn up, but because bureaucrats were too busy trying to protect their own programs from attack by other bureaucrats (1979, 5). Bureaucratic politics in the African sense is about conflict. For a long time in Africa, conflict has been justified as a means by which some powerful individuals and interests try to protect their communities, people, agencies, and domains. One way this is accomplished is that various powerful entities form their own parties whose aim is to cater to the needs of their own people. The ultimate objective of these parties is to use every type of maneuvering technique possible to secure resources for their people and agencies.

Political maneuvering has therefore become a tool often found in states with multiparty systems. Of course this is expected because the more parties or factions that are formed, the greater the chances of finding persons with political maneuvering skills. Considerable literature has developed around the issue of political maneuvering. The reason for this is that political power brokers use their political maneuvering skills to amass wealth for themselves while claiming to represent the interests of the powerless. Also of interest is that a network of clientelism has developed whereby powerful lords/leaders solicit the loyalty of a large number of masses while promising these people a decent means of livelihood (LeMarchand and Legg 1972).

F. Communications/Public Relations Skills

Conceptually, the communications/public relations skill category is defined as the management of communications between an organization and the public. From a general standpoint, communications/public relations involve the ability of bureaucrats to clearly convey organizational purposes to the broader society, both for political support and policy implementation. For our purposes, the cluster of activities representing communications/public relations skills include knowledge of community relations, the ability to communicate, knowledge of public relations, and the ability to exhibit leadership traits (Montgomery 1986C).

Communications and public relations skills have been identified as instrumental to community development (Deutsch 1961). Monte Palmer, for instance, noted that in order to build cooperation between the bureaucracy and the public, administrative officials must be able to properly convey their intention to the clients whom they serve (1985, 273-274). In the US, Harold Gortner, Julianne Mahler, and Jean Bell Nicholson (1987) suggest that success in government depends upon the attitude held when dealing with the bureaucracy, the legislature, the media, or the public. Romney stated that "to shape [the public's] attitude, there is a much greater need in government for the ability to communicate than exits in any business I can think of" (1987, 49). According to former United States Commerce Secretary Peterson, a department or agency employing personnel with the ability to articulate can use such communications ability to increase impact and effectiveness. Gortner, Mahler, and Nicholson contend that the "ability to communicate with the larger public and relate to the broader public serves as a catalyst, mobilizing the force of a vast unyielding bureaucracy and moving it toward the administration's goals" (1987, 51-52).

The Limits of Comparative Administration

Part of the underlying problem in comparative public administration is that the field has never had an embracing theory. Eric Welch and Wilson Wong (1998, 41) note that there are two traditions in the field. The first emphasizes the political, social, and economic context of different nations ("traditionalists"); the other emphasizes the characteristics of bureaucracy and compares these to universalistic phenomena ("revisionists"). Irving Swerdlow suggests that for development administration, "like public administration of which it is a part, it is a subject matter in search of a discipline" (1975, 324). Other scholars have pointed out that, indeed, the term development administration is not conceptualized in any precise and generally accepted fashion. The label, Siffin says, identifies a loosely sensed interest that exists because people deem it important; its significance does not depend upon a paradigm, nor does it depend on a systematic array of theoretical knowledge (2001, 6). In any event, the knowledge in and of development administration has a Western flavor, and is often difficult to apply in non-Western nations.

In a recent retrospective essay, for example, Ferrel Heady raised two issues regarding the comparative administration field. First, comparativists were eager to find a framework for analysis that would permit comparisons on a global basis. They had a special interest in the administrative problems of newly independent developing countries and they were confident that these problems could be dealt with by transferring administrative technologies from more advanced countries. Yet they were unable to agree on a paradigm for the field or a consensus as to how "scientific" their studies could claim to be (1998, 3).

In addition, Heady raised other common concerns for the field that include the following questions:

1. What is the best framework (or what are acceptable optimal frameworks) for the comparative study of national systems of public administration?
2. What are the current and prospective possibilities for achieving "scientific" knowledge about improvement in administrative capabilities in each of the above settings?
3. What are the major trends, prospects and developments in less developed nations?
4. How can a competent civil service operating in an inadequate administrative structure be achieved in international organizations, given the context of a global nation-state system?
5. What are the implications for comparative and international administration of possible future system transformation? (1989, 503).

The development of comparative and international administration was, and remains, influenced by Western ideas. As a result, theoretical development in the 1960s and 1970s reflects the application of Max Weber's typologies, Talcott Parsons' functionalist approach, Fred Riggs' prismatic model, and Ferrel Heady's bureaucracy approach. The need for many newly independent developing nations to modernize and rationalize their societies and institutions has led their leaders to look to Western countries to provide the model. This includes maintaining the functions of their political and economic systems as well as developing the managerial and institutional capacity needed for implementing development projects efficiently. One result has been the reliance on the Western model of development, but this model never has had theoretical hegemony: its assumptions have been challenged in a number of situations, including where the unique historical and cultural experiences of indigenous people were involved (Jun 1976).

More recent critiques of the comparative administration field suggest that to understand new international transformations, we need to transcend the conceptual orientations of rationalism, positivism, scientific research, and macro-theory because these cannot reflect changes that occur. By shifting our perspective to ways of understanding local conditions and social interactions, we should be able to develop deeper sensitivity to the potential for global, national, and local changes (Jun 2000).

A related criticism is that reliance on very rational, quantitative approaches places too much emphasis on the similarities and differences among countries. The literature in comparative administration for the past twenty years seems to suggest that scholars are shifting their interest away from the similarities among countries. Current trends in comparative research suggest an interest in the differences among countries in the areas of policymaking, institutional development, and administrative practices, to mention just a few. Charles Lindblom and David Cohen (1979, 115) suggest that if we grasp uniqueness as well as understand the tacit nature of administrative settings, then we may be able to gain knowledge that reflects the pluralistic nature of politics, institutions, and human actions. Others have suggested that through interpretation and through understanding differences, we can understand how a particular phenomenon, such as the psychological behavior of bureaucrats, centralized decision-making, or an organization's network is socially constructed as well as culturally and historically influenced. In other words, we can learn about the subjective nature of human conditions (Jun 1976, 144).

Another problem for the comparative field is the selection of criteria used in studying similarities and differences. The choice of largely quantitative techniques for data gathering, such as surveys, questionnaires, and tests to establish concepts and variables for comparative purposes leads to only a partial inclusion of relevant factors. In fact, context-specific characteristics that may be unique to a particular setting are often excluded from analysis. As a consequence, people's experiences and the meaning they place on the events, processes and structures in their everyday lives are neglected, calling any findings into question (Miles and Huberman 1994).

There is a tendency for academic disciplines to isolate comparative studies from other sub-fields because this represents a barrier to theoretical development and enrichment within these disciplines. Yet, in order to enhance understanding, it is crucial for the development of perspectives in those social sciences to examine each national experience in light of that of other nations. Doing so allows scholars to understand the effects that differences in structures, cultures, and values have on each other, and on the performance of the particular aspect of the social system that is being investigated (Peters 1990, 3).

Another limitation of the comparative administration field pertains to the tendency to extrapolate theory on the basis of a single national experience. Such an idiographic approach (Przeworski and Teune 1982, 4) has had rather unfortunate effects for theory development concerning public administration within the social sciences. For example, adopting such an approach further diminishes the chances of evolving anything approaching a paradigm for the study of public administration. This is particularly true involving a paradigm that would be applicable in settings other than where the study had taken place. Although a single paradigm may not be necessary, the absence of any successful and broad-based attempts at the development of such comprehensive approaches represents a major weakness in the theoretical development in this field.

Another factor that is worthy of mention is the perceived low level of development of the comparative administration field. All too often it has been asserted that the comparative study of public administration is perhaps the least developed aspect of the study of comparative politics and government, despite the long history of the field. For example, comparative administration was an essential part in the traditional approaches to comparative government. Several key reading materials in the field contain significant portions on administration and implementation of policies through the public organizations. Also, the comparative study of public administration had a central place in the 1950s, '60s and '70s as scholars attempted to understand the role of public administration in implementing development programs, as well as the differences in administrative behavior and its relationship to levels of development (Riggs 1976). As part of this low level of development in the field, comparative study of public administration has lagged behind its sister sub-field, the comparative study of public policy. The latter sub-field actually began as an explicit "sub-field" within the academic political science much later than comparative administration (Hancock 1983; Dierkes et al. 1987). Furthermore, several models and theories to explain differences in policy have been subjected to empirical testing. Overall, B. Guy Peters (1989) suggests that it is unfortunate, but also fair, to say that there has been something of an intellectual malaise surrounding comparative administration.

Finally, the approach adopted by many scholars and practitioners of development administration in the United States during the last two decades has been problematic. These models of administrative relations and behavior have resulted mostly in hierarchical relationships in several developing countries characterized by a lack of dialogue and a poor understanding of local conditions. (See Hyden, Olowu, and Okoth-Ogendo 2000).

The failure of technical assistance projects in many developing nations since the early 1970s raises questions regarding the administration of these models during the same time frame. Despite the good intentions of donor countries, many assistance programs produced uneven accomplishments because of a lack of commitment from both the host institutions and the general public, in addition to wasted resources, corruption, and limited institutional capacity. Much of this deficiency can be traced back to the methodological orientation undergirding the practice of comparative administration during the past three decades (Posz, Janigan and Jun 1994; Norgaard 1994).

One thing is clear: the field of comparative and development public administration is facing a crisis. As O.P. Dwivedi (1999) suggests, this crisis is precisely a consequence of the inability of developing countries, including scholars in the field, to incorporate the substance of other non-Western development experiences into the prevailing thinking about comparative administration. A comprehensive review of the literature of comparative administration shows that several challenges are occurring. While it is not possible to discuss all of those within the context of this chapter, five significant ones will be briefly highlighted here.

(1) Incorporating the Influence of Political Forces

In the developing countries, an absence of administrative and management approaches exists that blend political, economic, administrative, cultural and religious forces to produce the desired policy results. The practice of development administration assumed many

Western values, including the separation of politics and administration. The perception that management in the public sector would be dominated largely by administrators (since they are presumed to have the expertise in formulating and designing economic plans for achieving national goals) was evident. It was also assumed that there was no place for the political dimension in the administration of development. Much of this thinking may be consistent with observations made by Coralie Bryant and Louise G. White in *Managing Development in the Third World* (1982). In their book, Bryant and White discussed the paradox of development administration within the context of underdevelopment and incapacity. According to these authors, the paradox of development administration is that effective administration is essential to accomplishing development, and yet its very effectiveness can also stifle and inhibit political development.

Part of the problem of development administration is seen in the historical experience of colonialism. A colonial state was the administrative state par excellence. Colonies were administered to rather than governed; resources were managed with goals of the colonial power in mind. At issue is the exercise of control, which requires the effective administration of scarce resources whether or not this meant the expansion of access to decision-making about those resources. However, administration also was the necessary element to enhance the capacity of locals to determine their own futures. Overall, the paradox suggests that as administrators develop their capacity to manage resources, they are likely to halt the expansion of political institutions that are essential to further distribute power more broadly (Bryant and White 1982, 25).

In fact, as the Iran experience, among others, demonstrated, in developing countries politics could not be kept separate from economic planning or the management of resources in the public sector (Dwivedi 1999). Or, as Merilee Grindle (1980) notes in *Implementation of Public Policy in the Third World Countries*, either the administrative system responds to political demands, or the politicians and indigenous leaders simply bypass the established administrative system and create their own network to accomplish their objectives. It is suggested that by their nature, development issues are political because they deal with the authoritative allocation of values in the context of limited resources. So therefore, in the developing countries, public sector management cannot be expected to remain purely within the realm of value-free administration (Dwivedi 1999).

(2) Imitative or Indigenous?

Ferrel Heady suggests that there was a tendency for countries, including those that escaped Western civilization, to put into place some version of modern Western bureaucratic administration. Such a model, he pointed out, was usually patterned after a particular country's experience, with key features borrowed from another country. The range of nations that had colonies in the developing countries included Great Britain, France, the United States, Spain, Portugal, Belgium, and the Netherlands. While the style, form and extent of administration imposed by these colonial countries may have varied, the fact remained that outside influences have largely shaped most of these developing bureaucracies. As a result, the bureaucracies remain quite imitative because they reflect values of the countries and cultures from which they were drawn. What is often lacking in these models is flexibility in making adaptations as conditions change, particularly to enhance the legitimacy of these bureaucracies and to point them toward the effective accomplishment of developmental goals (Heady 1991, 297-298).

(3) Shortages in Administrative Skills

Public bureaucracies in developing nations continue to be deficient in the requisite skills necessary to carry out developmental programs. Part of the problem has to do with unemployment and underemployment. Many public services in developing nations tend to be overstaffed in the lower ranks with attendants, minor clerks, and other cadres. The actual shortage is in trained administrators with management capacities, developmental skills, and technical competencies needed to accomplish administrative chores. In response to the paucity of available administrative and managerial skills, analysts paint a very bleak picture. According to Heady (1991, 299), for example, "given the disparity between minimum needs and maximum possibilities for meeting them, there is no short-range solution to the problem of administrative capacity in most new countries. Even if the public bureaucracy succeeds in recruiting most of the available talent, this only diminishes the available supply for political parties, interest groups, and other organizations in both public and private sectors."

(4) Emphasis on Non-Productive Activities

Third World nations are often accused of engaging in activities that are not production-oriented. This means significant bureaucratic activity is channeled toward the realization of goals other than the achievement of program objectives. Fred Riggs refers to this as "preference among bureaucrats for personal expediency as against public-principled interests." This behavior is most prevalent when deep-seated values are carried over from a more traditional past, which has not been modified or abandoned despite the adoption of non-traditional social structures. A good example of this is the value attached to ascription rather than achievement. Most developing countries emphasize status, and status relationships are the prime motivating factors, rather than program goal achievement. Hence, there is an emphasis on the relationship between status and goal achievement as a way to foster change in those bureaucracies.

This orientation has several implications for the practice of administration in the developing nations. According to Riggs, one area that is greatly affected is in "bureaucratic recruitment" where the choice for official personnel processes predominates. Associated with this concern are issues of nepotism and favoritism. This practice makes it likely for a top level official to select people for employment whose loyalty he or she trusts. It also opens the door for the possibility of choosing from family and friends whose confidence the top official has. And, to cap it all, such non-merit considerations greatly influence promotions, assignments, dismissals, and other personnel actions within the service, as well as the conduct of affairs with agencies' clientele on the outside (Riggs 1964, 230-231). Additional dimensions of this problem include issues of corruption that may range from payments to petty officials for facilitating a minor transaction to bribes at higher levels (Caiden, Dwivedi, and Jabbra 2001).

(5) Discrepancy between Image and Reality

An important characteristic of administration in developing nations is the widespread discrepancy between form and reality, a phenomenon Riggs (1964) has labeled as "formalism." Conceptually speaking, formalism is the tendency to make things seem more as they presumably ought to be rather than what they actually are. Examples of formalism, or the gap between expectations and realities, abound: enacting laws that cannot be enforced; adopting personnel regulations that are quietly bypassed; announcing a program for delegation of administrative discretion while keeping tight control of decision-making at the center; or reporting as actually met production targets which, in fact, remain only partially fulfilled. As Heady (1991) rightly concedes, these tendencies are present in developed countries such as the United States, Japan, France, and others; however, such acts are more frequent and have greater consequences in most of the developing countries.

Contending Theories of Development

Two dominant concepts—modernization theory and dependency theory—have characterized the study of development (Riggs 1964; Chilcote 1974; Rostow 1965; Huntington 1968; Galtung 1971; Wallerstein 1975; Valenzuela and Valenzuela 1978; Deutsch 1961; dos Santos 1970; Frank 1966). Because the discontent with these approaches has spurred more critical ideologies, we end this chapter by first providing an overview of these two core theories, and then outlining the basic themes in development public administration as a prelude to the discussion of interpretive approaches in the next chapter.

Modernization theory was a philosophy that grew out of a perception that government can contribute positively toward social progress. For example, in the United States, the government mitigated the effects of the Great Depression of the 1930s, successfully mobilized and managed the war economy of the 1940s, financed and supervised the Marshall Plan partnership that restored the shattered economies of Western Europe, and guided the unprecedented and sustained economic growth of the 1950s and early 1960s (Galbraith 1958). These examples demonstrate that big government can be regarded as the beneficent instrument of an expanding economy and just society. As many nations gained their independence in the 1950s and 1960s, the idea that this model could be applied with similar results was eagerly adopted. It was also thought that only through proactive government could what came to be known as the Third World countries be redeemed from poverty and ignorance.

In an attempt to show how development was fostered in the newly independent Third World countries, Walt W. Rostow (1965) saw the process of change as a series of stages through which each nation passes. According to Rostow, Great Britain was the crucial example since it was the first state to embark on the evolutionary path into the modern industrialized world; the inference was that this path was a model to be copied by other nations.

Rostow's theory describes five stages that should lead to development:

1. The traditional society where agriculture is the basis of power

2. The preconditions for "takeoff," which is a transitional stage where land is no longer the basis of power and there is infusion of technology that is supported by resources raised from the land

3. The "take off," when a new class of entrepreneurs emerge, technology

expands into agriculture and commerce, profit is reinvested, and the quality of life rises because production is now expanded

4. The drive to maturity where there is sustainability, and output outstrips population growth, when more sophisticated industries are established

5. The age of high mass consumption characterized by increased resources that are allocated to social welfare/security, and the development of the welfare state

Rostow's stage theory has been criticized as being terribly misguided at worst because development is greatly influenced by time. As an example, when the developed nations were in the early stages, they had for the most part secure political, administrative, social, economic and cultural bases. The experience of the Third World nations is totally different since they do not have their basic institutions in place, and their entrepreneurial and administrative capacities are weak to nonexistent. Overall, Rostow's model is considered to be too deterministic as a practical guide for development (Esman 1974, 3-26; Huntington 1968).

There were two themes in modernization theory that reinforced the notion of big government and the salience of development administration as a moral and intellectual vocation. The first was the universality and inevitability of the spread of Western values and practices— instrumental rationality, secularism, individualism, and science-based enlightenment—to all areas and peoples of the world (Black 1966; Riggs 1957). The hope was that modernization would convey to the late "developers" (that is, Third World countries) the same benefits, just as inevitably as it already had in Europe and North America. In effect, development administration was to represent a complex of insights, skills, and practices that could facilitate modernization and thereby help to vindicate and universalize America's moral responsibility to share its technical achievements with those less fortunate.

The second theme of the modernization paradigm derived from the elitist bias. The agents of modernization would be the enlightened minority who had acquired Western education and were committed to transforming their societies along Western lines. This transforming minority would work out of urban centers, and collaborating with the government, they would rationalize economic life, expand the modern centers, help improve the quality of everyday life, and gradually penetrate the traditional institutions of the rural periphery through the state bureaucracy. Overall, public administration would be the principal instrumentality by which the modernizing elites would bring about change (Esman 1988).

This functionalist approach, which emphasizes the need to adopt the elements of a modern bureaucracy in order to develop, has been a prevalent mode for characterizing comparative and development administration since the 1960s. Adoption of this approach might also have been a consequence of its parent field, public administration (Wilson 1887). It proceeds from the assumption that organizational efficiency and productivity can be achieved through the application of scientific method and a set of management principles that place heavy emphasis on hierarchical command and strict adherence to work rules, budget control, planning, systems analysis, efficient allocation of human resources, and recently total quality management (Bryant and White 1982, 33). The functionalists put their emphasis on the structural and functional coordination among administrative units and on organizational adaptation to the environment. An important assumption is that because people are by nature rational and self-interested, human motivations and behaviors are predictable and can be empirically explained by testing a set of hypotheses and examining casual relationships. It assumes that social reality is already created by external forces and that rational explanations can be given. Based on this approach, all that needs to be done is to measure and uncover the truth by determining casual relationships that exist in objective reality. Finally, it adopts a deductive approach to change, seeing it as a set of principles to bring about and guide action (Jun 1993, 47-48).

Furthermore, modernization theory suggests that culture, traditional attitudes, and institutions stemming from the colonial experience have proven to be a serious and fatal stumbling block to any indigenous efforts for Third World countries to develop economically, socially, and politically. That is, values, institutions, and patterns of action of traditional society are an "expression" and "cause" of underdevelopment and are obstacles to modernization (McClelland 1963). In a large-scale study entitled *Becoming Modern,* Alex Inkeles and David Smith (1974) explored the psycho-cultural factors influencing development. They concluded that underdevelopment is a state of mind. Based on an "overall measure of modernization" they determined the extent to which participants in their study exhibited the characteristics of the modern man. The authors discussed the implications of the presence or absence of such modern men in a given society and went on to argue that modern attitudes produce modern behaviors that are essential to development. They concluded that without modern men, modern institutions are bound to fail.

Dependency theory argues that a number of factors account for the underdevelopment of Third World countries. These factors include the colonial experience, terms of trade, financial markets, military assistance, development assistance, and foreign aid, just to mention a few. Dependency theory rejects the modernization view that the appropriate unit of analysis is the nation-state. Furthermore, dependency theorists argue that the cultural and institutional features of a country are not the key factors explaining its backwardness and underdevelopment, but are rather intervening variables only.

Theotonio dos Santos identifies three basic forms of dependency—colonialism, financial-industrial, and multinational corporations—limiting the development potential of newly independent nations. He goes on to suggest that these new forms of dependence restrict the size of local markets and contribute to income inequality in developing countries (dos Santos 1970; Umeh and Andranovich 1992).

According to Samuel Valenzuela and Arturo Valenzuela (1978, 543-557), the dependency perspective assumes that the development of a national or regional unit can only be understood in connection with its historical insertion into the worldwide political-economic system, which emerged with the wave of European colonization of the world. This global system is thought to be characterized by the unequal but combined development of its different components. Among others, Andre Gunder Frank (1966) notes that underdevelopment and development are aspects of the same phenomenon, occurring simultaneously and linked functionally. This results in the division between industrial, advanced, or "central" countries, and underdeveloped, backward, or "peripheral" countries. Dos Santos (1970) adds that the relationship between these countries, with the dependent countries placed in a backward position from being exploited by the dominant countries, needs to be a key point in analysis.

Immanuel Wallerstein reinforces the position articulated by dos Santos and others. Considered as the driving force behind the "world systems" school of thought, he explains the existence of the gap between rich and poor countries by arguing that all states form part of the capitalist world economy. In the world, the existence of differences in wealth is not an anomaly but rather an outcome of the fundamental processes driving the economy. In this view, the gap between rich and poor ultimately will disappear, but only when the capitalist world system that has been in place since the sixteenth century itself disappears (Wallerstein 1975).

Today, the debates in development administration research tend to focus on four facets of development management. Derick Brinkerhoff and Jennifer Coston (1999) describe these four elements as a means to foreign assistance agendas, as tool kits, as values, and as processes. Just as the theoretical shift from modernization theory to dependency theory and other critical approaches has altered the conceptual terrain, it has also altered the practical terrain. While institution building in the bureaucracy and capacity building for project planning, based on technical, rational, and universally held assumptions once held sway, we now see an administrative reorientation toward the integration of politics and culture in management education, participatory service planning and delivery, and community capacity building based on a more sensitive, politically infused, multisectoral and multiorganizational model (Brinkerhoff and Coston 1999, 348-349). These authors point out that development management requires accepting multiple agendas (for example, of aid recipients and donor organizations); using a variety of management and analytical tools; and valuing self-determination, empowerment, and the equitable distribution of benefits in society. The process highlights the importance of political and value issues to development (1999, 349). The next section expands the discussion of these issues, which we believe are central to establishing the rationale for using interpretive approaches in comparative public administration.

Some Common Themes in Development Public Administration

A number of accepted themes have emerged uniting the interests of scholars and practitioners that provide the basis for informed dialogue and mutual criticism and learning. If development is conceptualized as an increase in the capacity to influence the future, then there are certain consequences for development administration. First, it means paying attention to capacity; that is, to what needs to be done to expand the ability and energy for change to occur. Second, it involves equity considerations, or the fair distribution of benefits and opportunities among prospective clients. Third, it means participation in the sense that only if people feel empowered will they receive the benefits of development. Fourth, it means taking seriously the interdependence in the world and the need to ensure that the future is sustainable (Bryant and White 1982). Fifth, it involves effectiveness considerations—toward the degree to which public services actually reach clients and achieve their intended objectives. Sixth, it involves efficiency considerations—the most favorable ratio of costs to outputs in the range of choices open to the program administrator. Finally, it involves stability considerations—establishment and maintenance of means for the peaceful accommodation of competing interests among parties affected by development administration. According to David Fashole

Luke (1986, 75), these themes, or persistent trends as he refers to them, constitute a continuing challenge to the efficacy of Third World countries caught in the management of the development process.

A. Building Administrative Capacity

Capacity in government is the process of identifying and developing the management skills necessary to address policy problems. It includes attracting, absorbing and managing financial, human and information resources, in addition to operating programs effectively, and evaluating program outcomes to guide future activities (Rondinelli 1983; White 1987). In Third World nations, as in the industrial nations, this process requires the assessment of an organization's capabilities at three levels: managing intra-organizational relations (internal bureaucratic affairs); managing inter-organizational relationships (affairs in the agency's organizational environment); and managing the broader political, economic and social relationships within which the agency operates. The specific skills necessary to accomplish these varied management tasks are neither easily identified nor routinely implemented. In effect, it is important to look not only at the particular administrative organization, but also more broadly at the political, social, and economic systems within which that organization functions. In many Third World nations both the traditional and transitional institutions add layers of complexity to the tasks of public administration and management.

It should be noted that the identification of administrative management skills depends on the specific functions required of the government administrators. In other words, the skills depend upon the job at hand. Managerial roles tend to have internal and external dimensions, such as meeting standard operating responsibilities as well as developing implementation strategies. Although the internal dimension is often the topic of interest (how are management decisions made?), the external dimension often raises the most difficult questions. This can easily be seen in queries of concern to development administrators (practitioners) and public administrationists (scholars). How will the development plan be put into practice? How are communities to be mobilized? How is development to be implemented? According to Bryant and White (1982), the presence or absence of needed skills at appropriate levels—the question of capacity—often explains why development is such an elusive phenomenon (Umeh and Andranovich 1992).

B. Citizen Participation

Citizen participation is an attitude of openness to the perceptions and feelings of others; it is a concern for what difference a project makes to people's lives; it is an awareness of the contributions that others can bring to an activity (Bryant and White 1982). Popular participation is an important dimension in the administration of public services. Within the context of development administration, participation involves the relationship of career administrators to both citizens and the public interest. Participation, in the more active sense, involves exerting influence on administrative behavior and on the outputs of official action. For example, greater participation by the poor and deprived would mean their ability to have greater influence on decisions and programs relating to their quality of life. Hence, there is a need to distinguish genuine participation, which implies real influence, from symbolic, manipulated, or controlled participation, which is intended to ratify rather than influence official behavior (Montgomery and Esman 1971: 359; Arnstein 1969; Friedmann 1992).

A resounding theme in the literature is the dissociation from the 1960s models in the administration of public services. These presumed bureaucratic hierarchies delivered prepackaged goods and services to the public according to classical bureaucratic rules in the context of prevailing center-periphery relations. Subsequent and more contemporary research and reflection suggests that, for development activities, responsive behavior from the affected public is required if services are to be accepted and if they are to produce the intended behavioral changes, including investments of time and resources.

C. Decentralization

Decentralization of political and administrative authority is often thought of as a necessary institutional arrangement for the maximization of public welfare. This includes the actual empowerment of local government to create and undertake programs for community betterment (Michie 1989). A widely accepted definition of decentralization is provided by Dennis Rondinelli, John Nellis, and Shabbir Cheema (1984, 18-25). They explain that decentralization can be defined as the transfer of responsibility for planning, management and resource raising and allocation from the central government and its agencies to

(a) Field units of central government ministries or agencies,

(b) Subordinate units or levels of government,

(c) Semi-autonomous public authorities or corporations,

(d) Area-wide, regional or functional authorities, or

(e) Nongovernmental private or voluntary organizations.

Decentralization is a multi-dimensional concept consisting of the redistribution of administrative responsibilities within the central government from headquarters to field/local administration; the delegation of decision-making and management authority for specific functions to semi-independent agencies such as public enterprises, regional planning and area development authorities, multi-purpose and single-purpose functional authorities, and special project implementation units; and "debureaucratization," or the facilitation of decision-making through political processes that involve political interests rather than through the usual channels (Rondinelli, Nellis, and Cheema 1983, 18-25).

Overall, decentralization can be seen as a way of increasing the effectiveness of development activities by making them more relevant and responsive to local needs and conditions, allowing greater flexibility in their implementation, and providing a means of coordinating the various agencies involved at the regional or local level (Conyers 1983, 99-100).

D. Responsiveness and Accountability

Administrators are confronted by several challenges and dilemmas as they try to be responsive to the needs of the public. For example, questions arise such as: which groups or members of the public should be included in decisions; to whom should administrators be responsive, to the organized public or the unorganized and less visible public; what is the best way to evaluate citizen preferences when they contradict professional training and judgment; and what can an administrator do if organized citizens either veto or dilute a project so that little is done (Uphoff et al. 1979).

While the above questions regarding access, responsiveness, professionalism, and effectiveness tend to assume that administrators want to be available to the public involved, this assumption is not always accurate. Citizens may easily be manipulated by administrators who feel primarily accountable to their own agencies or supervisors. As a result, the public's primary agenda is to hold administrators accountable and to find some ways to influence them. Correspondingly, accountability is particularly important precisely where political institutions are weakest (Bryant and White 1982, 212).

Overall, a top-down/bottom-up flow of communication and initiative seems to be recognized as the main ingredient in responsive and accountable administrative capacity. The tendency for policymaking to be highly centralized in a national administrative structure is further acknowledged as a major constraint on attempts to meet these goals.

E. Equity

Development includes distributional issues. To the extent that only a small segment of the population benefits from the outcome of development, it has not occurred. On a broader scale, development is a normative concept implying that ensuring more equity in access and benefits is a value in itself (Bryant and White 1982, 16).

This normative dimension of development administration focuses on social justice demands, especially in the context of severe scarcity. It demands that resources and efforts must be concentrated on improving the life chances of those groups in society not particularly well placed to help themselves. Accordingly, the Brandt Commission (Brandt 1980, 49) echoed Pearson (1969) in asserting that:

> Development is more than the passage from poor to rich, from a traditional rural economy to a sophisticated urban one. It carries with it not only the idea of economic betterment, but also of greater human dignity, security, justice, and equity.

Summary

Clearly, the values in public administration and the values in development sometimes clash. While there isn't a clear-cut appropriate way to organize a government service or a correct path to development, what should be clear from this review is that it is not enough to suggest one way of approaching an administrative challenge. We agree with Paul Steidlmeier's conclusion (1987, 165) that the complex interaction between culture and development has not been given enough attention. This is the topic of the next chapter.

Chapter Three

The Interpretive Dimension of Administration

Culture and its Impacts

This chapter presents an exploratory mapping of the use of culture as a tool for examining administration in Africa. We are particularly interested in the nations of southern Africa, which are among the poorest in the world. Our interest stems from the generally low-level performance that has resulted from a number of programs, most of them externally implemented, which have focused on capacity building in the region. Why haven't these programs been more successful? We believe that a general lack of consideration of local context, in fact more specifically, the consideration of local culture, has played an important role in undercutting these capacity building efforts.

As an exploratory mapping exercise, this chapter uses the literature to identify the elements of local culture that should be taken into account when considering public sector performance, and then draws out how these elements of local culture impact performance.

The Case for an Interpretive Approach to Administration

As a backdrop for making the interpretive case, we will quickly recap some of the assumptions underlying development administration. The logical positivist approach has been the prevalent mode for the study of administration ever since the publication of Woodrow Wilson's article entitled "The Study of Administration." This approach proceeds on the assumption that organizational efficiency can be achieved through the application of scientific methods of research. It assumes that because people are by nature rational and self-interested, human motivations and behaviors are predictable and can be empirically explained by testing hypotheses of cause and effect relationships. It also assumes that social reality has been already created by external forces and that rational explanations can always be given. Based on this approach, all we need to do is to measure and uncover the truth by determining causal relationships that exist in objective reality (Jun 1993, 47-48).

The interpretive approach, in contrast, has emerged as a reaction against positivist, or deterministic, assumptions implied in modern management theories and behavioral sciences. Because of different historical circumstances and values, particularly in non-Western regions of the world, many of the assumptions made in the preceding paragraph are not accurate. While this has not slowed the use of frameworks anchored to Western values, it has led to the search for alternative frameworks that more clearly illuminate the historical conditions that underpin the formation of political and administrative processes we wish to understand.

In all this, it is the "tacit" dimension of administrative practice that becomes important, the understanding of how culture, language, symbols, and objects are interpreted in and through administrative action. A key argument of the interpretive mode is that human actions and motivations are not conditioned by external demands, but rather are the result of an individual's interpretation of the meanings attached to external elements, such as organizational tasks, hierarchical relations, functions, roles, and so on (Silverman 1970). For public administration, these interpretations are understood to take place within a given institutional or cultural context (Schon 1983). Edward Hall (1959, 52), for example, concludes that culture controls our lives in "many unsuspected ways." What is critically important in this formulation is that culture hides more than it reveals. It is this hidden dimension of administrative activity that interests us.

It can be further argued that the adoption of an alternative interpretive method in a comparative context helps to reveal variations in public administration, including differences in analyzing policies, institutions, and administrative practices. According to Lindblom and Cohen (1979), if we grasp uniqueness as well as understand the tacit nature of administrative settings, then we may be able to gain knowledge that reflects the pluralistic nature of politics, institutions, and human actions. In addition, through the examination of variations and differences, we can better understand how a particular phenomenon, such as the pathological behavior of bureaucrats, centralized decision-making, or administrative networks, is socially constructed as well as culturally and historically situated. Overall, the promise of using interpretive approaches has the potential of capturing more of the complexity and nuances inherent in administrative practices.

Public Administration in the Non-Western Context

Significant differences exist between developing and developed countries in terms of the nature of the relationship between their overall administrative systems on the one hand, and their economic, political and cultural contexts on the other. Such differences are largely due to the fact that while the administrative arrangements in the developing countries reflect their exogenous (both colonial and post-colonial) origins, the administrative systems in Western capitalist nations represent their endogenous societal contexts.

For instance, in terms of the economic context, public bureaucracies in the advanced capitalist nations are quite compatible with their traditions of limited state intervention in the economy, reliance on the institutions of competitive market forces, and a complementary relationship between the state and private capital. However, in most developing countries, the inherited or borrowed Western models of bureaucracy are often incompatible with their economic contexts characterized by limited market competition, expansive state intervention and market guidance, in addition to conflicting state-capital relationships (Haque 1996, 315-316; Heady 1991).

Shamsul Haque describes the incompatibility between the administrative elites and the common people on the one hand, and the formally expected behavior and actual administrative actions on the other. These types of contradictions are a reflection of a more microlevel mismatch between the exogenous cultural values inherent in the administrative realm and the indigenous cultural values found in the developing societies (Haque 1996, 322).

Judging by the findings of several studies, this phenomenon is common among developing countries. With regard to Arab countries, for instance, Jamil Jreisat suggests that cultural values are frequently incompatible with critical elements of the purely rational and impersonal characteristics of bureaucratic management. According to Jreisat, the underlying values of the Third World bureaucracies mostly represent various foreign sources, including the colonial administrative heritage, post-independence administrative reforms based on

Western models, and knowledge of Third World experts trained in Western institutions. These types of values, he suggests, are inconsistent with indigenous values in the developing countries. In sum, because of these exogenous origins, the administrative values are different from, and often in conflict with, the deeply ingrained traditional values found in the Third World (Jreisat 1991, 672).

In fact, other scholars have attempted to put the significance of cultural variables rather more poignantly. According to O.P. Dwivedi and Keith Henderson, administrative policies in Third World countries go beyond the rational bureaucratic values, and are often influenced by cultural assumptions based on race and ethnicity. The point here is that the indigenous cultural values have an impact on the administrative systems; the idea of value-free public administration is a myth rather than a reality; and that the borrowed Western administrative models have been incompatible with and ineffective in non-Western societies holding different sets of values (Dwivedi and Henderson 1990).

According to Milton Esman, the context surrounding Western modernization included three factors that do not hold for other countries which became politically independent after World War II or that failed to industrialize before that time. First, the Western nations had a reasonably secure political base for modernization. Major governmental and political structures were in place, and a sense of national identity linked individuals and intermediate groups to the political system. There was legitimacy in governance, and political processes produced non-bureaucratic groups who were competent to govern. Western administrative systems were characterized by a separation from politics, instrumental efficiency, and the organization of public organizations in hierarchical structures. This guaranteed the primacy of lawmaking over administration, which was limited to the pursuit of political goals and by the control of superiors over subordinates in the bureaucracy. Second, in the Western nations there were widespread entrepreneurial (and other) capabilities which were called on to perform a variety of developmental functions. Many of these activities were entrusted to voluntary organizations and local governments. As a result, this limited the financial and organizational burdens on the state and its agencies. Third, societal demands for public services, though they appeared to be intense at the time, were modest and well within their capacities to handle (Esman 1974, 3-10).

In terms of the cultural context, the normative features of modern bureaucracy such as merit, competition, specialization and impersonality have been compatible with Western values including secularism, individualism, rationality, competition, profit motive and advisement orientation (Baker 1991; McClelland 1961; Weber 1958). In the Third World context, such bureaucratic norms are often contradictory with extant cultural values such as ritualism, ascriptive norms, caste structure, informality, extended family, seniority-based authority, collective responsibility, and so on (Dwivedi and Nef 1982; Haragopal and Prasad 1990).

Conceptualizations of Culture

As a framework for understanding, culture has been studied extensively; as a result, myriad conceptions of it abound. The following excerpted definitions are from forty-five books and articles on organizational culture and closely-related subjects. While they are representative of the literature, they are neither exhaustive nor listed in any particular order of importance.

Organization culture has been defined as: symbols, language, ideologies, rituals, and myths (Pettigrew 1979); behavioral regularities (Goffman 1959, 1967; Van Maanen 1979); patterns of interactions, values, and attitudes, which are derived from traditions, precedents, and past practices and are most visible in the team formations within which managers work; the assumptions and beliefs people live by (Blake and Mouton 1969); and beliefs, practical syllogisms, justifications for behavior (Morley 1984). Others point to core values that determine the organizational philosophy or mission (Selznick 1957); organizational climate, attitudes toward work, degree of personal responsibility for work (Lippit, Langseth, and Mossop 1985; Miles and Schmuck 1971; Tagiuri and Litwin 1968); patterns of cognitive processes (Weick 1979); and speech, communication patterns, language, nonverbal communication (Everd 1983; Meissner 1976). Culture refers to myths, anecdotes, and stories (Cohen 1969); stories that control organizations (Wilkins 1983); a belief in and a commitment to excellence (Peters and Waterman 1982); the organization's ethic, for example, the pubic service ethic (Buchanan 1975); values and norms (Tichy and Ulrich 1984; Hall 1977); symbols, language, and art (Hayakawa 1953); and the sources of norms, rules, group attitudes, customs, and roles (Wharton and Worthly 1983). Culture also underpins the degree of consensus on general values; organizational goals; means, policy, and tactics; commitment to participate in organizations; performance obligations; cognitive perspectives (for example, common language, shared frame of reference, and an agreed upon set of canons for empirical testing) among the different status groups in the organization (Etzioni

1975); and is the who's who, what's what, why's why of an organization's informal society (Barnard 1968). Others see culture as a mind-set in the realm of feelings and sentiments, the basic values, assumptions, or expectations that have emerged from the organization's particular history, leadership, and contingency factors supported by present-day management policies and practices; also worldview and beliefs, meanings and symbols, historical vestiges, traditions, and customs (Allaire and Firsirotu 1985).

Organizational culture can be thought of as the glue that holds an organization together through a sharing of patterns of meaning. Culture focuses on the values, beliefs, and expectations that members come to share (Siehl and Martin 1984, 227); the customary and traditional way of thinking and doing things (Jaques 1990); rituals and ceremonies (Smircich 1983); the pattern of shared beliefs and values that give the members of an institution meaning, and provide them with the rules for behavior in their organization (Davis 1984, 1); and values, heroes, rites and rituals, and communications.

A strong culture is a system of informal rules that dictate how people are to behave most of the time (Deal and Kennedy 1982, 15); the set of important assumptions, often unstated, that members of a community share in common (Sathe 1985, 2); a pattern of basic assumptions invented, discovered, or developed by a given group as it learns to cope with its problems of external adaptation and internal integration that has worked well enough to be considered valid. These patterns, therefore, are taught to new members as the correct way to perceive, think, and feel in relation to those problems (Schein 1985, 9).

A standard definition of culture would include the system of values, symbols, and shared meanings of a group including the embodiment of these values, symbols, and meanings into material objects and ritualized practices. Culture governs what is of worth for a particular group and how group members should think, feel and behave. The tools of culture include customs and traditions, historical accounts (be they mythical or actual), tacit understandings, habits, norms and expectations, common meanings associated with fixed objects and established rites, shared assumptions, and intersubjective meanings (Sergiovanni and Corbally 1984, vii); the link between language, metaphor, and ritual and their celebration of particular social ideals or myths form the essential administrative culture of the school. Culture is a translation of myths into action and relationships (Bates 1984, 268).

In a cross-national study involving forty independent nations, Geert Hofstede (1980) concluded that many of the differences in employee motivation, management styles, and structures of organizations throughout the world could be traced to differences in the collective mental programming of people in different national cultures. According to Hofstede, culture can be defined as the collective mental programming of the people in an environment. Culture, he suggests, is not a characteristic of individuals, it encompasses a number of people who were conditioned by the same education and life experience. For example, when we speak of the culture of a group, a tribe, a geographical region, a national minority, or a nation, culture refers to the collective mental programming that these people have in common contrasted to other groups, tribes, regions, minorities or majorities, or nations (Hofstede 1980, 43). The study suggests that we are all conditioned by cultural influences at many different levels, including family, social group, geographic region, and professional environment.

As part of this large-scale study, Hofstede attempted to determine empirically the main criteria by which national cultures differed. Four such elements were discernable, and they included the following dimensions: power distance, uncertainty avoidance, individualism-collectivism, and masculinity-femininity. For instance, power distance was meant to indicate the extent to which a society accepts the fact that the power in institutions and organizations is distributed unequally; uncertainty avoidance indicates the extent to which a society feels threatened by uncertain and ambiguous situations and tries to avoid these situations by providing greater career stability, establishing more formal rules, not tolerating deviant ideas and behaviors, and believing in absolute truths and the attainment of expertise. Individualism-collectivism as the third element can be described as follows: Individualism implies a loosely-knit social framework in which people are supposed to take care of themselves and their immediate families only, while collectivism is characterized by a tight social framework in which people distinguish between in-groups and out-groups; they expect their in-group (relatives, clan, organizations) to look after them, and in exchange for that they feel they owe absolute loyalty to it. Measurements in terms of the masculinity-femininity dimension express the extent to which the dominant values in society are masculine—assertiveness, the acquisition of money and things, and not caring for others. These values were labeled masculine because in nearly all societies, men scored higher in terms of the value's positive sense (assertiveness) than of their negative sense (lack of assertiveness) even though the society as a whole might veer toward the feminine pole (Hofstede 1980, 45-46).

In an extensive study exploring the influences of organizational culture and learning in public agencies, Julianne Mahler (1977) explored the direct effects of the role of culture on interpreting performance results, informing the meanings inscribed in established routines, defining what constitutes legitimate information, specifying the consideration to be given to external demands, and defining subculture relations. In pursuing the influence of culture, she raises important probing questions: How does culture influence the interpretation of the events that we expect will stimulate learning? What meanings do organization members draw from apparent disasters and triumphs? How do commonly held beliefs as revealed in myths about the true meaning of the organization, legends about past successes or failures, or stories about the identity or prowess of its officials influence the interpretation of prominent or conspicuous events as problems to be remedied, or situations to be accepted resignedly, or opportunities to be taken? What meanings are invested in existing routines, and how do members react to challenges to these routines?

What do organizational rituals, argot, or often told stories symbolize about the meanings of particular routines, programs, or procedures? What do rituals connoting, for example, the scientific or humanitarian character of agency work to tell us about how officials will respond to particular criticisms of program paradigms? What does the cultural content of programs and entrenched routines suggest about the kinds of problems that will be recognized or how debates about alternatives will proceed? To what kinds of program changes would it even occur to officials to give serious consideration? How do rituals surrounding the transmission or communication of information affect the credibility of the information or other aspects of its interpretation?

For instance, language and visual displays are artifacts that can reveal much about the organizational identity of officials. They can also help explain why some channels of communication are valued over others, influencing what kinds of reports will be seen as convincing (Mahler 1977). Furthermore, how does the organization socialize officials to deal with outsiders, such as clients, oversight institutions, interest groups, other agencies, or local residents? How does the collective frame of reference about actors in the external environment influence the level of attention or inattention that particular outsiders receive? What kinds of needs, requests or demands will officials see and put on the agenda for change? Finally, what impact do hostile subcultures have on the spread of reforms or innovations? How do the norms of a subculture influence the interpretation of information from other admired or despised groups? (Mahler 1977, 534).

Culture, then, is one of the basic theoretical lenses in the social sciences. It entails a very high level of abstraction. Culture is not obvious until we have learned to recognize it, and it is something we will never encounter on the ground (Ingold 1994; Shapiro 1970). Other scholars in the field have also defined culture as actor, action and result or as content, process and effect. As content, Edward Taylor (1924) suggests that culture, or civilization, taken in its wide ethnographic sense, is the complex whole that includes knowledge, belief, art, morals, law, custom, and any other capabilities and habits acquired by man as a member of society. Karl Weick (1995) and Edgar Schein (1985) would add that culture is shared experience. As process, culture has been defined as ways of learning and knowing or collective cognition (Mintzberg 1990); and as a system to send, store, and process information (Elashmawi and Harris 1993). Tim Ingold went further to suggest that people live culturally rather than live in cultures. And, as effect, culture includes the placing of a system of constraints and limits on individuals (Pfiffner and Sherwood 1960); the development of a collective perspective, or the learned product of group experience (Schein 1985; Nonaka and Takeuchi 1995).

Finally, in an important genre of research, culture was used in at least two senses: First, as an idealized cognitive system of knowledge, beliefs and values that exist in the minds of individual members of a society, and second as a collectivity of persons sharing this ideational ordering of their reality (Cason 1981, 7).

In public administration, the inner workings of the public sector can be better understood by focusing on its social and cultural elements. For instance, what are some of the subjective meanings that administrative phenomena have for public administrators? Elements such as feelings of loyalty, obligation, harmony, conformity, and caring are not apparent and cannot be understood merely from institutional and objective viewpoints. It is hoped that by examining these tacit and subjective phenomena, the cultural characteristics that distinguish African administration from that of other countries can be discerned. As we explore some of the cultural elements, we can see that the interpretive approach can be used as a method that will significantly enhance the degree of understanding and appreciation of the dynamics of administration within the ranks of the developing southern African countries.

Culture and Public Administration

Our reading of the literature points to the need for incorporating culture more centrally in the study of comparative public administration. In the case of the nations in sub-Saharan Africa, this is a challenge of conceptualization. For instance, what is culture and how does it impact public administration? While the definition of culture may be said to be a pattern of behavior specific to a period or a people, unfortunately, as an analytical concept, culture is not easily operationalized. In large part, this is because culture is a dynamic concept. Political scientists, for example, tend to discuss political culture as a paradigm, yet the ongoing conflict and contestation of "the political" means that culture is often the product of a struggle (Chabal and Daloz 1999). Indeed, Durham (1999, 212) notes that because a society has a common political culture, this does not mean that it is "intransigent, homogeneous, and consistent." Much of the discussion that follows will be based on cultural variables synthesized from the literature.

African public bureaucracies, like their counterparts in other countries, are structured in a bureaucratic manner, with hierarchy, specialization, rules and regulations, complex structures, technology, and so forth. The central questions that are all too often raised regarding African public bureaucracies are: How are decisions made in the bureaucracy? How are public employees able to cope with their complex work environment? To what extent does traditional culture influence the behavior and actions of public employees? Much work has focused on the first two questions, with the third question typically answered, "It is an obstacle." However, there has been recent renewed interest in this third question.

Osabu-Kle argues that understanding culture is the key to the future development of democracy in Africa. Getting there requires establishing culturally compatible political preconditions, a task that is different in Africa than in the West. His analysis begins by differentiating between Africa and European politics. African politics stems from a culture of cooperation and compromise, and competition plays a destructive role (2000, 74-75). Prior to colonial times, the representation of different African clans on ruling councils provided opportunities for bargaining and reconciliation. But with colonialism and its institutional trappings, politics became more difficult. Political parties were established on top of existing communal divisions within African societies, and one result is that it has become much harder to create a climate for bargaining and reconciliation. Furthermore, given the different cultural basis for societal decision-making in Africa (consensualism rather than individualism, cooperation rather than competition), the circulation of elites is not as important as gaining the input of all elites (75).

Patrick Chabal and Jean-Pascal Daloz argue that the failure to understand that many of the concepts used to analyze Africa, such as democracy, multi-party elections, and political culture, have in fact been Africanized leads many analysts to misread performance. Rather than concluding that Africa can't or won't modernize, Chabal and Daloz demonstrate that Africa works in different ways than Western societies. In addition, the role of the state, and the relationship between state and society, is different. Chabal and Daloz argue there is a built-in bias toward greater levels of disorder and against the formation of Western-style legal, administrative, and institutional structures necessary for development. One of the keys to better understanding Africa is to realize that in the present time, cultural dynamics should be examined from the modern instrumental uses; that is, Africa's present circumstances encourage the creative use of "the traditional" (1999, 147), and should give analysts pause before they draw unwarranted conclusions.

Despite the fact that it is difficult to conceptualize culture, some specific black (American) cultural features have evolved (Bishop 1977; Howard 1977; Ford 1978; Giordano 1976). In a study examining the implications of black culture for public administration in the United States, Charles Sanders operationalized components of black culture for the purpose of studying their impact on public administration. The first of these is black character. He suggested that blacks value naturalness, spontaneity, and authenticity in a context of group sharing. A second component is black faith. He suggests that blacks value commitment, purpose and humanistic advocacy within the context of religious and group action. The final component is black righteousness. He suggests that blacks value equity and justice in a context of respect for themselves and others. In Sanders's view, these features, that is, high values and attitudes among (American) blacks make black culture distinctive; these have been powerful forces for the survival and enhancement of black people. He goes on to argue that these features are powerful tools that can be used toward the improvement of the practice of public administration systems (Sanders 1980, 33). In his view, the application of black naturalness, spontaneity, authenticity, group sharing, commitment, purpose, humanistic advocacy, equity and justice to administrative systems will lead to new and different management styles in which more equitable, involving, and humanizing administrative practices take place.

Interpreting the Cultural Components of Administration in Africa

According to Wesley Bjur and Ashgar Zomorrodian, if we take the position that public administration can be an ecological (or contextual) phenomenon rather than merely a generic (or universal) phenomenon, then administrative theory would refer to conceptual descriptions of how the administrative system is organized, how functional roles and relationships are defined within the institutions responsible for achieving societal goals, and how people are engaged in such functions and relationships within the organization. Also, within a particular cultural setting, theory itself is based upon a set of culturally influenced assumptions about how things work, from which managers regularly make interpretive inferences affecting decisions and actions. For these authors, cultural views are incorporated in these assumptions, which in turn color the administrator's understanding of administrative processes and dynamics, including how to respond in the organization's interests. Furthermore, cultural values give a particular form to every nation's administrative institutions, and, through them, influence issues of general concern to administrative theories. Cultural assumptions, they maintain, dictate the proper expression of individual and organizational goals; determine how an organization's mission is to be legitimated; and how structural, functional and behavioral relationships in the organization are to be worked out (Bjur and Zomorrodian 1986, 399-400).

There is no shortage of material in the contemporary literature supporting the importance of culture in the study of public administration. In one genre of research, culture was used in at least two senses. First, as an idealized cognitive system of knowledge, beliefs and values that exists in the minds of individual members of a society, and second as a collectivity of persons sharing this ideational ordering of their reality (Cason 1981, 7). Michel Crozier (1964) discussed how French culture affected supervisory and employee behaviors in two state monopolies. He pointed to the strong sense of hierarchy stemming from traditions within the family, and an avoidance of face to face confrontations in favor of rule resolution of conflicts in the administration and operation of those organizations. Other works which provide examples from East Africa and Asia of cultural traits that distinguish these societies from others include Moris (1977) and Hofstede (1980). Also, the writings of Pondy and Mitroff (1979), Louis (1980) and Deal and Kennedy (1982) represent a different genre of literature proposing the importance of cultural perspectives to the study of organizations and their administration.

Because culture is known to inform "sense making" (Louis 1980, cited in Shafritz and Ott 2001, 377) and interpretation of the kinds of ambiguities seen in puzzling data, problematic situations, uncertain program technologies, and obscure links between problems and solutions, it becomes useful to consider some particular ways that culture influences administration. More specifically, how certain elements of the African societal culture may influence administrative protocol and what is being administered. Culture has most often been seen as a source of resistance (Schein 1985) or a source of defensive routines to learning and change (Argyris 1991). Schein suggests that it might be worthwhile to consider the more creative potential of culture as a basis for the interpretation of situations and experiences that could prompt learning and the construction of effective solutions (Mahler 1977, 520). Culture, including the derivatives of culture or what Amil Cabral (1979, 141) refers to as cultural manifestations, influences the capacity of the bureaucracy to learn and helps determine the direction that learning will take.

Without comprehending the cultural or hidden dimensions (Hall 1963; 1987) that define African societies, it is difficult to attempt to understand the factors that influence the conduct of public administration in those bureaucracies. Understanding African culture, including the meanings embedded in those cultures, is essential in order to fully understand why African public administrators behave the way they do in carrying out their work. Furthermore, an understanding of African culture serves to clarify the reasons for the discrepancies that are often discernible between the practice of public administration in the African context and in the Western world. It is important to underscore the fact that the African cultural components (or traditions) that have been identified above, where positive, contribute to the viability, and thus the stability of African societies and their bureaucracies. This viability/stability factor is critically important in sustaining a reliable cadre of public servants (public administrators) who are usually charged with the implementation of policies that are made whether under a military or a civilian regime.

Strong empirical evidence exists to suggest culture has important consequences for the structuring, management, and behavior of organizations in both developed and developing nations. Seen as social institutions, both public and private organizations have a tendency to take on the cultural attributes of the societies in which they operate

(Inzerilli and Laurent 1983; Rieger 1987; Hofstede 1980). Culture and cultural studies are important because they provide a better understanding of the context within which organizations and the management process take place (Kiggundu 1989, 31). What follows is a more pointed examination of the relationship between African culture and these cultural factors that influence the conduct of public administration in the African context.

Most Third World countries have inherited or borrowed a Western administrative framework that emerged in a Western cultural context. As a result, bureaucracies in developing nations represent the continuity of roles and attitudes drawn from a previous colonial heritage; the patterns of their own local cultures remain significantly different. Scholars such as De Guzman et al. (1991, 5) suggest that Western administrative techniques have been introduced without regard to their acceptability and consistency with prevailing mores, customs, values, and norms in the target community.

Administrators in the developing countries are not totally free from the influence of local contexts, and as a result they themselves often encounter conflict between the formal or expected administrative behavior based on Western bureaucratic norms and expectations. This tension between formal official rules and actual activities and conduct often leads to ritualism or formalism in different aspects of the administrative system (Riggs 1964). A considerable degree of this formalism or ritualism can be observed in the major bureaucratic activities and attitudes in the developing nations.

In many ways, much of African society may still be characterized as a vertical or male-dominated society (Hofstede 1980), one in which most human relationships are based on a person's hierarchical position, status, educational background, seniority, and gender. The old African-style relationship between master and servant or older and younger has today been transformed into the relationship between administrative director and administrative assistant, manager and subordinate, and senior and junior. In much of Africa, most public servants, no matter what their organizational status, recognize the existence of senior and junior relationships. Within the context of the work environment, two employees (in the senior and junior cadres, respectively), can establish a highly paternalistic and trusting relationship simply because both individuals had, for instance, attended the same educational institutions, or were colleagues in some capacity prior to joining the present organization. Such a personal relationship with another individual who has the same educational, regional, occupational, or social connections may not only influence one's intra-agency activity but also one's inter-agency relationships when seeking advice, political support, or information. A senior-junior relationship is a two-way relationship. One who chooses to violate this basic norm is likely to be poorly regarded by others. They might experience diminished respect from friends, and may jeopardize future dealings with superiors and colleagues who may have attended the same institution. In short, how an individual manages his or her personal relationships and maintains stability in the bureaucracy may be dependent on a number of factors: one's hierarchical position, status, educational background, seniority, and gender. As a result, one of the most important qualities of a higher public servant in an African bureaucracy is the ability to establish personal relationships with both junior and senior level counterparts. Another quality may be the ability to work with other people, remaining sensitive to the needs of employees, including their emotional problems, which may include job stress, anxiety, or even family matters. If, for instance, an employee experiences stress because of a heavy workload, the manager feels a sense of obligation to redistribute part of that employee's work to other employees.

In Africa, workers inherently feel a sense of obligation when they receive a work assignment from their manager. The downside to this is that sometimes this same employee may be experiencing great difficulty carrying out the job, but feels reluctant to seek help or give the assigned task to another worker out of shame and humiliation. Sharing assigned work responsibility with another may be viewed as an inability to organize tasks, use time efficiently, or carry out the task diligently. For this reason, a manager or supervisor needs to monitor work assignments amongst his or her workers. In fact, as Jong Jun and Hiromi Muto noted in their study of subjective meanings in vertical relationships in Japan, an effective manager is someone who cares about the needs of employees. The employees will, in turn, demonstrate their respect for a caring supervisor. In Africa, the types of relationships we have described are viewed as one of mutual interdependence, not of domination and subordination: the success of one party in the relationship is said to depend on the support of the other (Nakane 1970, 74; Doi 1973).

The Role of Economy of Affection

Goran Hyden suggests that there have been few studies that have attempted to measure the quantitative and qualitative impact of the "economy of affection" on a national economy in a given country. The reason for this is partly due to the nature of this phenomenon, and also its intractability. While the anthropological literature provides examples of such efforts, very little attention has been paid to their impact on society. Yet, the literature on urban life in West Africa suggests that cultural, religious, and other such organizations fulfill important functions. As part of his study, Hyden discusses three categories for understanding the functional purposes of the economy of affection in Africa.

To arrive at a better understanding of the social, economic, and cultural realities surrounding public administration in Africa, Hyden suggests that it is helpful to examine the functioning of the peasant mode of production, otherwise known as the economy of affection, that functions side by side with the prevailing economic system in many countries (Hyden 1983).

Economy of affection, according to Hyden, denotes a network of support, communications and interaction among structurally defined groups connected by blood, kin, community or other affinities such as religion. In this type of communal system of production, household units cooperate for both productive and reproductive purposes. This type of cooperation, according to Hyden, is not an inherent and permanent part of the production system; it tends to be ad hoc and informal rather than regular and formalized. Although these entities may appear invisible since they may not be referred to as organizations in the real sense, and because they make no direct contribution to macroeconomic factors, they may represent opportunities and obstacles in the development effort to foster change in the African region. The economy of affection is most prevalent in the rural community but it is also an integral part of society at large. Its influence stretches from the grassroots to the apex of society. We turn now to a discussion of the aspects of the economy of affection that appear to be relevant to the present discussion.

The three components of the economy of affection are: basic survival, social maintenance, and development. To some degree, these components have implications for social change and transformation, particularly in public administration. Because the economy of affection tends to cater to people who feel that they are only peripherally involved or feel marginalized by the market economy, the economy of affection provides a mechanism for support and survival. A key aspect of this mode is the face to face nature of exchanges. Along with this is the sense of trust and mutual obligation that makes the bulk of Africans feel inclined to give priority to arrangements of an informal rather than a formal kind. Some examples of these may involve the exchange of cash as in the case of a poor rural peasant receiving cash from a friend or relative, goods such as food or clothing, or services such as labor or child care. Although these types of exchanges may be nominally limited to a few individuals at a time, taken together they perform an extremely important function in society that formal institutions cannot match. Given the orientation described above, it will not be unusual to find that workers with a worldview colored by the economy of affection will be more inclined to engage in more face to face transactions since doing so will allow them to establish trust and a sense of obligation with their fellow workers and perhaps their supervisors as well.

The second category is social maintenance, an activity that spans from gift giving within small circles of relatives to contributions for religious or political purposes. Examples of these include offering hospitality to relatives and friends in need, companionship, and the provision of loans. Hyden suggests that it also includes sometimes vast expenses that people are prepared to incur in conjunction with ceremonial functions like weddings and burials. However, as Hyden notes, these social maintenance activities may produce consequences that are anti-developmental. In an actual case cited by Hyden to illustrate this phenomenon, it became very clear that the microevent of the economy of affection tended to get priority over the macroeconomic perspective on development. It also demonstrated how the economy of affection tends to prevail over formal sector concerns with development.

From a developmental standpoint (which is also the third category), it would be fair to say that a considerable part of the product of the economy of affection is private goods and benefits, whose contribution to collective goods should not be ignored. Activities undertaken under the rubric of economy of affection fall under what is often referred to as informal sector activities and may include efforts such as farm purchases and farm development, promotion of small-scale business, house construction, support of education, facilitation of migration, and community development. These are all efforts undertaken by small groups of people to help enhance the quality of life for themselves and others. As Hyden puts it, much community development in Africa has been carried out under the auspices of local groups that are mobilized through the application of given affection criteria (Hyden 1983).

The development capabilities of groups such as these have important implications for public administration. In an environment where resources are very scarce, the role of the economy of affection becomes extremely important, as it can become an important source of strength for public administration. For example, public administrators would need to find creative and effective strategies for not only working with members of these small groups, but also harnessing some of the strength they bring with them. In this regard, notions such as co-production and empowerment come to mind as a means of evolving a collaborative process of governance at the local level in the community.

The foregoing section has been devoted to an interpretation of how the economy of affection provides a safety net for the many poor, and how it also serves a developmental role by diverting surpluses generated by the formal economy to be used by people who do not have formal access to structures of lending or other forms of investment. The economy of affection also has the effect of holding back development by delaying changes in behavioral and institutional patterns capable of sustaining economic growth at the national level.

There are aspects of the economy of affection that have been deemed to be counterproductive. First, it is suggested that the economy of affection imposes social obligations on individuals that limit their interest and capacity to support public concerns outside of their communities. To be clear, there is often over concern with meeting immediate, extended family, and clan-related obligations so that there is hardly any time and resources left to devote to national and superordinate matters of national importance (Montgomery 1987). This occurrence is largely due to the subsistence nature of the local village economy, including the absence of structures that create opportunities for people to rise above their present circumstances. As part of the cultural reality, the few who are better off find themselves in a situation where they are overwhelmingly expected to provide for the welfare and sustenance of numerous family members. This phenomenon exists partly because the notion of a welfare system is nonexistent in the African context, and so responsibility for providing for one's extended family system falls on the shoulders of the few who are able to do so. Hyden refers to this occurrence as the perpetuation of the locale-specific outlook by people on development issues and concerns.

A second manifestation of the negative side of the economy of affection is the existence of tribalism and nepotism in hiring practices. In small, non-formal rural environments, tribalism and nepotism may have served to bring people together that shared common origins and purposes. However, as societies grew larger and became more diverse with people who espouse different religious, political, social, economic, and especially cultural orientations as part of the same community, the importance of these practices has been terribly diminished. These issues are not necessarily peculiar to African developing countries; Western industrialized nations have had to deal with them as well.

And, more importantly, in large-scale, formal organizations that are based on Western models of administration or management, such practices are very difficult to justify. But what does this glimpse behind the curtain of culture suggest about other ways that culture informs development administration?

Chapter Four

The SADCC Studies

This chapter undertakes a re-assessment of the most compre-
hensive study of public administration and management in
Africa, a project conducted by the United States Agency for
International Development (USAID) and the National
Association of Schools of Public Affairs and Administration (NAS-
PAA) involving the then-nine nations in the Southern African
Development Coordinating Conference (SADCC): Angola,
Botswana, Lesotho, Malawi, Mozambique, Swaziland, Tanzania,
Zambia, and Zimbabwe. Based on that large-scale study, several
research articles were published in the scholarly literature. As a
prelude to our re-examination of a subset of those studies in
Chapter 5, this chapter contextualizes the previous SADCC studies through a meta-analysis of the framework, methodology, and
findings of existing studies (Przeworski and Teune 1982). In particular, we re-examine the premises established and the conclusions drawn in each of those studies with an eye toward seeing the
extent to which "culture" enters into the research design or helps
explain findings and conclusions in an attempt to determine how
some of those conclusions can benefit from an "interpretive" re-interpretation or perspective. Building on our arguments in the previous
chapter, it is our contention that greater insights could have been
gained had the cultural dimensions been made an explicit part of
the SADCC project.

In pursuing this effort, our presentation consists of two main parts.
First, we provide an in-depth discussion of the methodology used in
eliciting the critical incidents data that are the basis of the SADCC project

and the research papers stemming from it. This is followed by a presentation of the findings of the eight published studies that have resulted from the SADCC data. Then, in the second part of the chapter, we re-examine the findings from these studies, paying careful attention to see whether or how African cultural values might underlie these findings. Overall, it is our view that when the original SADCC project was conducted, and when present-day researchers have used the SADCC data, the lack of attention or sensitivity to the cultural/interpretive context of public administration in Africa has yielded an incomplete picture of the practice of development administration, particularly in addressing why certain outcomes in administrative performance have occurred.

The SADCC Methodology

As an overview, a variety of methodologies exist through which data is collected for comparative analysis. These range from traditional positivist methods, including survey research and elite interviews, to post-positivist methods such as participatory workshops. The conduct of the large-scale SADCC study used a unique type of data collection that blended these different approaches: critical incidents regarding management events.

In 1984, NASPAA, with funding from USAID, launched a major study of management training needs in the nine member countries of the Southern African Development Coordinating Conference. Rather than adopting traditional research techniques, a critical incidents methodology was employed (NASPAA 1985; Fivars 1980). This methodology is primarily based on a collection of written events. An "event" is something that actually has taken place. For example, respondents were asked to briefly describe the last situation in which they praised a subordinate, or in which they last made a major error on the job. This method should not be confused, however, with the survey technique, which is intended to elicit information about opinions and which, when used to generate conclusions characterizing large groups, has to rely on statistical sampling techniques to prevent distortion in the findings.

The management events collected for the SADCC project, rather than the managers themselves, were considered to be the basic unit of analysis. The method used in gathering the management events is derived from the "critical incidents" procedure that was developed during World War II in order to determine whether and how training and organizational changes could improve the performance of combat pilots. In the critical incidents method, the most recent experience of the respondents is gathered. These are considered random in the sense that the selection of events requires respondents to cite the most recent incident in their experiences. The critical incidents procedure has been employed thousands of times for purposes of studying human performance in different situations (private, professional, military, and civilian; Flanagan 1949, 419-425; Fivars 1980).

The reported events gathered in the SADCC research project provided a unique database that described the actual behavior of individuals on the job in nine countries, including some who worked for private concerns, some who were government employees, and some who were members of parastatal organizations (our interest is only in the government employees). The events were selected out of participants' experiences, not because they represented any supposedly unusual features but because they had occurred most recently in the respondents' managerial lives. In this sense they were random, current, and derived from personal experience rather than from hearsay or ideology (Montgomery 1986B, 7).

The critical incidents data set, specifically aimed at identifying skills needed in the region, gathered reports of management events from government administrators who were invited by their own governments to participate. The research design of the critical incidents methodology in the SADCC project took the following form. The first step was a general interview of public and private officials by the study team during a scheduled site visit. At the time of the initial interview, ten permanent secretaries, managing directors, or deputies were invited to complete a short management events diary listing five or six events that occurred over a period of five to ten days. The public officials worked in large civilian ministries that conducted training (for example, Health, Personnel, Economic Affairs, Finance, Education, Minerals and Water, Local Government and Lands, Agriculture, Labor and Public Service, Communications, and Trade and Industry; Montgomery 1986B, 212). Then in a separate setting, a questionnaire was administered to groups of officials at different organizational levels in conjunction with a training exercise, or at an official meeting dealing with organizational issues usually held in the capital city. This questionnaire asked for a brief 20 to 50-word report describing a specific event associated with a positive or negative managerial experience. Each of the 1,865 management events in this data set was coded according to one or more of nearly 50 identifiable skills. These data identified the administrative and managerial skills used in the conduct of development public administration in these nine nations, and whether the use of a particular skill resulted in the successful resolution of the reported incident. When the skill led to effective management practice, it was coded "positive;" otherwise, it was coded "negative."

The SADCC Management Events Codebook

Because of the complexity of the data, a manual was developed to assist with data management. The manual provided guidelines for the classification of the management events using codes established for the SADCC study. The management events or critical incidents were classified according to the particular management skill each illustrated. Below are the definitions of each skill category used in the SADCC study (NASPAA, 1985). We present these descriptions to show that the SADCC project, while focused on management training and education, identified and then coded the management skills involved in each critical incident using fairly traditional Western oriented public administration values.

1. Accounting: Professional level of skill in designing systems and keeping records of financial transactions in such form as to meet internationally recognized standards of accuracy and reliability.

2. Drafting and Writing: Ability to present an official case clearly and effectively in official documents and other correspondence. It includes skills such as organization, clarity of expression, and coherence of argument.

3. Research: The ability to support a position on an issue or support current operational demands of an organization by investigating and bringing to attention key aspects of an issue. It is related to skills such as policy analysis, and negotiations.

4. Rules, Regulations and Procedures: Knowledge of rules, regulations and skills in interpreting and adapting them to accommodate the current operational needs of an organization.

5. Policy Analysis: Skills relating to the understanding of both (rational) decision-making and (proto-rational) implementation processes and the manner in which these two aspects interact to form policy. These skills are related to skills of impact assessment and community relations.

6. Legal Knowledge: Skills related to the understanding and awareness of the law and its relation to one's task, programs and organizational environment.

7. International Negotiation: Knowledge of conflict resolving approaches and the ability to use these and other procedures to bring about collaboration between transnational actors.

8. Political Environment: Pertains to skills in handling local politicians, party politics and ideology. These skills are separate from the skills in handling the politics of resource allocation and turf fights, which are more appropriately classified under bureaucratic politics.

9. Supervision: The skill of supervising and supporting the performance of subordinates without infringing on their sense of dignity and their independence and creativity as a member of an organization. Sometimes this skill category may overlap or be related to issues and skills pertaining to motivation or to improving the use of an organization's resources.

10. Work Scheduling: The ability to determine priorities in assigned tasks and to allocate time for them so that the essential functions are performed before activities of lesser urgency are undertaken.

11. Personnel Management/Administration: Skills in recruiting, assigning and compensating employees in an organization in accordance with its internal policies. It is related most frequently to issues concerning employee transfers, employment policies, salary policies, supervisory skills, and human relations problems.

12. Time Management: Skills pertaining to the efficient use of time. It is also related to skills in coordinating tasks, functions and responsibilities among different individuals and/or entities so that these are carried out in a timely fashion.

13. Management Information Systems: Skills in handling and ensuring the timely and accurate flow of information, intra- as well as inter-organizationally.

14. Motivation: The ability to encourage subordinates to perform effectively, using both job-related and employment environment factors to improve and stimulate enthusiasm. It is usually illustrated by events where employees show initiative and deal better than expected with a problem event; its absence or poor motivation can be inferred from ineffective performances from subordinates.

15. Organizational Management: Skills pertaining to restructuring an agency or other organization, and setting goals for an organization.

16. Expatriate Management: The ability to encourage or extract a desired performance level from expatriate personnel or foreign agencies operating within the country.

17. Delegation of Authority: The ability to size up the task environment of an organization's mission and to allocate assignments that accord with each individual's skills and resources, primarily in order to release scarce managerial time for tasks that require one's personal attention.

18. Typing and Secretarial Skills: Professional level of skill in secretarial tasks such as typing, filing, shorthand and other tasks related to the office.

19. Job Planning: The ability to plan future tasks, restructure assignments in a manner that enhances the individual's or organization's ability to accomplish the goals assigned.

20. Negotiations (in both peer and inter-organizational situations): Knowledge of conflict resolving approaches and the ability to use these and other transactions or procedures to bring about inter-organizational collaboration. It pertains to the ability to encourage different parties to agree to contribute needed input in order to accomplish a particular task or goal. It is clearly connected with the skill of coordination.

21. Financial Management: Ability to make effective use of an organization's monetary resources and to keep track of such uses. It is seen most often in relation to budgetary matters. This category also refers to the ability to provide or devise timely financial support for a program or project.

22. Technical Skills: Knowledge of auto mechanics, computer maintenance, nursing procedures, office techniques or other special subjects required for effective performance of organizational missions. It refers to particular skills not otherwise mentioned in any of the other categories.

23. Interpersonal Relations: Understanding the processes by which individuals working in a bureaucratic setting can cooperate with each other to achieve organizational goals. It is the ability to get along with co-workers and individuals in other organizations. Its absence is illustrated in personality conflicts, and favoritism.

24. Bureaucratic Politics: The ability to ascertain the divergent interests of various organizations and individuals that work together in matters of common policy, and to find ways of accommodating them without sustaining injury to one's own organizational or personal interests. It refers to events that reflect/imply the maneuvering that takes place whenever different organizations or individuals within the same organization compete for resources and/or

authority. It should be applied to events relating to how organizations negotiate with each other over turf and how individuals protect their perks within an organization.

25. Public Relations: The effective use of communication skills to promote a program, project, organization, or position.

26. Training: The ability to detect present and future deficiencies and introduce education in different skills to correct this.

27. Community Relations: The ability to develop a positive working relationship with the community where a project or program is implemented and recruit beneficiary participation within that community.

28. Project Planning: The ability to analyze and anticipate local needs and conditions, and structure the project components in accordance to those needs and conditions. The category is related as well to policy analysis and program analysis, since sound project planning depends on these latter two skills.

29. Resource Allocation: Ability to reorganize workers, goods, and services to decrease operating costs within an organization.

30. Communication Skills: Knowledge of the resources available to an organization to extend information to other users, and the ability to employ these resources effectively. It also refers to the ability to convey organizational goals effectively to those outside an organization.

31. Contract Management: The ability to handle contracts for goods and services as well as people.

32. Corruption Management: The ability to detect and terminate situations where individuals are acting contrary to the organization's, the program's or project's goals and rules.

33. Coordination: The skill of bringing together the resources, both human and material, of different individuals or organizational units to accomplish tasks common to the participants. The ability to coordinate functions among various departments of an organization and among different organizations sharing responsibility for the implementation of projects or programs.

34. Organizing Skills: The ability to structure special purpose units to carry out unusual events or activities that evade routine procedures and require the collaboration of various units. This includes activities not foreseen or provided for in the original project blueprint, but which are related to and enhance program, project or policy goals.

35. Contingency Management: The ability to cope with the unforeseen, with last minute changes in practices and procedures in order to accomplish the assigned task.

36. Disaster Management: The ability to put together and implement an efficient set of programs to deal with a catastrophic event such as a drought, flood, or epidemic.

37. Program/Project Analysis: The ability to structure programs or projects that reflect national policy goals as well as local idiosyncrasies and needs.

38. Impact Analysis: The ability to gather and effectively utilize knowledge pertaining to the outcome of the program or project on the community and the nation. It is related to evaluation/monitoring skills.

39. Data Analysis: The ability to transform raw data in a manner that provides useful information for the individual or the organization. It is related to statistical skills.

40. Economics: Knowledge of economic theory and the ability to apply that knowledge to increase the effectiveness of the agency's projects or programs.

41. Math/Computational Skills: Skills in arithmetic, but not directly related to accounting or finance.

42. Evaluation/Monitoring: The ability to devise techniques to follow up on project implementation and use the information gathered through such monitoring activities to enhance project performance.

43. Inventory Management: The ability to organize the acquisition and provision of goods and services in a timely fashion.

44. Language Skills: The study of other languages and the ability to use that knowledge to improve performance or solve problems.

45. Inter-organizational Relations: The ability to maintain cordial working relations between various organizations operating in one area or project/program.

46. Miscellaneous: Any events that do not reflect any of the preceding skills are assigned this code.

47. Management Adaptation: Ability to apply methods or techniques that have proven successful as solutions or improved performance in other environments.

48. Leadership: Generate and sustain followers, particularly subordinates,

and the ability to encourage them to try a new approach related to problem solving or operations.

49. Contract Negotiations: The ability to negotiate or renegotiate external (such as between agencies or with an outside entity) contracts or internal (such as within the department as with the workers union) contracts that are favorable to the company/organization/ division.

50. Initiative: The ability to perceive the need for a particular action and then accomplish the task (for example, an improved operation plan).

The SADCC management events derived through the critical incidents methodology have been used extensively since they were gathered in 1984. John D. Montgomery, in a series of research articles, used the SADCC management events for the following purposes: to investigate what the African manager does or should do on the job (1985); to improve administrative management in southern Africa (1985B); to examine the kinds of activities managers perform when they are engaged in bureaucratic politics (1986A); to understand and draw inferences about the exercise of managerial leadership in southern Africa (1986B); to examine the functions of permanent secretaries in nine southern African countries (1986C); to explore the relationship between Africa's political and cultural environments and its effect on managerial behavior and administrative systems in Africa (1986D; 1987A); to identify the administrative skills needed in the southern African countries, including how African managers serve developmental goals (1987B); and to explore the external strategic environment of public managers in developing countries, that is, the extent to which public managers need the support of a whole network of outsiders to achieve their major national goals (1991).

Similarly, Ogwo J. Umeh employed the SADCC data to explore differences in administrative characteristics among seven developing African countries (1990), and subsequently to examine the determinants of administrative development in seven southern African countries (1991). Then, Umeh and Greg Andranovich used the SADCC data to assess capacity building and development administration in southern African countries (1992), and finally, these same authors examined the linkage between the conduct of managerial work and its performance in these countries (2001).

The SADCC management events were used in a comparative study with events gathered in India to examine the kinds of issues with which the African and the Indian managers are most likely to be concerned

(Singh 1986). The data set was also used by Richard Vengroff in a comparative study to assess management training needs and policy reform in the Central African Republic and in southern Africa, respectively (Vengroff 1988). Vengroff, Mohammed Belhaj and Momar Ndiaye used the SADCC events data to study the nature of managerial work in the African public bureaucracies (1991). We re-examine these studies in the second part of this chapter looking for how each study considered culture in the analysis of development public administration.

Although the SADCC events provided some valuable data and insights, the database does suffer from methodological and conceptual weaknesses (Vengroff 1990). Two methodological weaknesses involve the timing of the data collection and the make-up of the respondents. A third, more general problem was in the coding of the events, particularly with inter-coder reliability.

Regarding timing, there is the assumption that events identified are, in fact, random because they represent the most recent management activities on the part of the respondents. This fails to take into account the fact that certain management activities are not randomly distributed throughout the year. Budgeting, planning, and inventory management are examples of managerial events that may be associated with distinct periods of time during the year (Vengroff 1990). The timing of data collection may have had a major influence on the relative frequency with which these types of events appear in the data.

Second, the size of the sample of events and the number of actual respondents may be a crucial factor for analytical purposes. When a relatively small number of individuals are interviewed, the peculiarities of a particular position or individual can become magnified and appear quite important (Leonard 1991). In the case of the several countries in the SADCC study (Malawi, Swaziland, Angola and Mozambique), a few individuals drawn from a particular service or with a particular interest can grossly distort the findings for that country. This can occur if the individual is either very active in citing cases or somewhat reticent (the average number of events cited in the SADCC study was eight, but the range was from one to fifteen). Thus, rather than viewing management events in general, the methodology may be attaching undue weight to the experiences of relatively few individuals. Finally, there is the issue of inter-coder reliability given the nature of the data (that is, written events) and the number of skill categories (50) and coders (20).

Conceptually, the skill categories, although linking process with performance (positive or negative outcomes indicating the relative effectiveness of management), tend to adopt a tool-oriented, Weberian focus. As others have pointed out, using a Western code of administration and a Western skills orientation masks important differences between how we in the West tend to think of administrative management and how African managers administer public affairs (Rondinelli 1983, 116-120; Jones 1989; Caiden 1991; Ronan 1993).

Research Findings of the SADCC Studies: A Meta-Analysis

Our thesis is that culture can play an important role in understanding public administration in developing countries. Given the fairly narrow focus of the SADCC study, our task in the remainder of this chapter is to determine whether, and how, culture was included by the authors in the studies noted above. We do so through a re-examination of the studies that resulted from the use of the SADCC critical incidents management events data. In particular, we examined each study in terms of the research question, methodology, substantive findings, and problems the author(s) noted, including any recommendations made, although not necessarily in this order. Finally, we engage in a re-assessment of those findings in an effort to determine the potential benefits of a "cultural" re-interpretation.

In the first study, "The African Manager," John Montgomery (1985) asked what tasks and functions African managers did as part of their work. He was also interested in exploring how performance could be improved among the rank and file of African administrators. Overall, Montgomery wanted to show the extent to which the management events data gathered from the southern African administrators reflected the presence of knowledge about current practice and future needs of public administration in the region. In order to get a clear sense of the extent of occurrence of each management skill in the events data, a frequency distribution analysis was conducted.

By running the frequency distribution analysis, it was possible to identify a rank order of most frequently used skills reported in the SADCC countries: motivating employees, personnel management, interpersonal relations, technical skills, writing skills, knowledge of procedures, financial management, negotiating skills, supervision, and bureaucratic politics. In addition, the ten least frequently encountered general skills were also identified: impact analysis, contingency management, inter-organizational, language, disaster management, program analysis, inventory management, computational, economic analysis, and community relations. Finally, the data was further disaggregated to separate the skills according to three managerial levels: senior, middle, and junior.

As part of the study's findings, by far the most important set of skills suggested by the SADCC management events involved the task of motivating subordinates to perform effectively. Another cluster of activities that constituted a coherent management function was the management of both human and physical resources. Third in frequency of appearance in the events recorded during the study were those involving both formal and informal organizational relationships. An important finding of the study for the purposes of education and training was that public services were seen as well administered, noteworthy in the early 1980s because the SADCC countries were still emerging and developing independent administrative practices.

A key problem Montgomery noted was the fact that there was a great shortage of managers and administrators, the presumed agents of both effectiveness and change in the African bureaucracies. The author lamented that most of the concerns the critical incidents reflected were largely internal to the organization (92).

Among other things, the author warned that it would be a mistake to place the entire burden of training design on the evidence of current practice. That is, to the extent that training is used to enrich the quality of management in organizations that are not well-managed, educational programs should not seek to perpetuate present styles of administration. Training, Montgomery suggested, is likely to be a more important factor in improving performance in the southern African region than in most other settings.

The goal of "Bureaucratic Politics in Southern Africa" (Montgomery, 1986A) was to examine in detail the kinds of activities that public managers perform when they are engaged in bureaucratic politics. For the purpose of this study, bureaucratic politics was defined as the efforts to influence the policies or behaviors of other organizations. According to the author, of the 1,800 management events in the SADCC database, 119 events were described as instances of bureaucratic politics; in other words, this was not a very large proportion of events characterizing the lives of these managers. These events were coded to distinguish between "processes" involved (such as appeals to a higher authority to resolve an inter-organizational conflict, as contrasted with direct negotiations, the use of intimidation, coercion, or positive incentives, or the surrender of a desired resource) and the "issue" that gave rise to the event (personnel matters, financial or other resource questions, problems of authority or jurisdictions, the performance of one of the organizations involved, questions of policy, and non-organizational or unofficial matters). The events were also examined separately for "improper behavior" to check on the validity of the common suspicion that bureaucratic politics are somehow reprehensible.

Overall, the findings pointed to the varied aspects of bureaucratic politics. Some situations permitted negotiations that circumvented regulations that would have produced problems for all concerned. Some situations seemed to call for the exercise of what in bureaucratic politics passes for "brute force." There were twenty-eight such cases, ranging from trivial to unimportant (apparently the sheer use of authority did not resolve important issues very often in the SADCC countries). Appeals to a higher authority provided the basis of another fifteen instances of bureaucratic politics. Like the "brute force" examples, the events show little evidence of negotiations or of compromise solutions.

What do bureaucrats "wrangle over" in southern Africa? Montgomery found out that the issues are money, turf, other bureaucrats, and policy. Funding was the most crucial subject matter in the bureaucratic events; twenty-nine incidents involved money matters. Turf, or jurisdiction was the occasion for twenty-five events involving bureaucratic politics such as personal relationships and organizational matters; twenty-one instances involved performance by other organizations that affected the success of other parties. Twenty-one instances also involved personal procedures or assignments and eighteen instances involved policy issues, or that the "absence of concern" over policy produced the incident. Finally, sixty instances involved issues of propriety—corruption, negligence, uncooperativeness, or lack of ability— that all led to conflict (409-410).

Montgomery noted that bureaucratic actors in the SADCC countries resolved issues on the basis of personal relationships often without attempting to build structural coalitions of like-minded partners. They did not consult their colleagues or attempt to formulate organizational positions prior to engaging in bureaucratic politics. He noted that when issues of turf and questions of policy arose, the response was defensive rather than proactive. He thought it was problematic that there was no sense of the "public interest" among the SADCC administrators (411).

The author did not make any clear-cut recommendations other than to caution that speculations made within the context of this study must remain impressionistic. All of this, according to the author, stems from the fact that "much of our present knowledge of bureaucratic politics is based on studies of large-scale crises involving political leaders" and the fact that "there is no third-world [sic] counterpart for Western studies on intelligence failures, missile crises, or foolish weapons decisions" (412).

In "Levels of Managerial Leadership in Southern Africa," Montgomery (1986B) examined the relationship between managerial behavior and motivation within the African bureaucratic context. He addressed the preconceived belief that motivation was (and still is) an important problem at all levels of management in Africa. The SADCC data also provided a basis for drawing some general conclusions about the exercise of managerial leadership even in routine situations. The importance of motivation was quite noticeable in the management events. In fact, in the SADCC countries, motivation came in first among all factors or skills identified in the management events. For instance, when the skills coded in the study were disaggregated to show the rank of the individuals involved, motivation appeared at the top of the list for all levels of responsibility, whether senior, middle or junior. It came in second in the incidents in which the respondent described an event in his most recent experience; first in the accounts of behavior of subordinates; second in the number of events in which the respondent was writing about the work of one of his colleagues; third in the situations involving the activities of a superior; and fourth in the cases in which the event transcended the internal workings of an organization because outside agencies participated. Overall, Montgomery found that perceiving and doing something about motivational problems is a managerial priority in all situations observed in the study.

A frequency distribution of the events data showed that the most persistent issues that emerged from the analysis of these incidents had to do with motivating subordinates (managers motivating other lower level managers in most cases). That function appeared in 377 situations, or 20% of the total number of events examined. The management events coded in the study were further disaggregated to show the rank of the individuals involved and the extent to which their activities had to do with motivation.

With respect to the African context, the study concluded that culture has a lot to do with the phenomenon of low motivation in the bureaucracy. According to Montgomery (1986B, 21-22):

> More serous problems are posed when the system itself
> has to be challenged in order to bring about a remedy.
> As might be expected, managers were much less

successful in dealing with systemic problems than in addressing motivational problems on a personal basis. Some African administrative institutions are deeply rooted, though "new" as aspects of an independent political system, and they often draw upon traditions far older than even the colonial period itself. Management events revealed the existence of a complex system of "ethnic arithmetic," by which tribal preferences took precedence over formal procedures for recruitment and promotion. Such behavior often appears mysterious and irrational to the outside observer, although its counterparts can be found in government operations everywhere. In the African situation, few managers were prepared to deal frontally with such issues, even if they were causing morale problems in their own staff.

Based on this observation, it is clear that culture (including ethnic preferences, tradition, and African endemic values) played an independent role in analyzing how African managers can motivate employees in the bureaucracy.

Overall, Montgomery concluded that the SADCC study shows that the exercise of managerial leadership in Africa involves more than the mere transfer of known principles; rather, it is beginning to display characteristics of its own (25). As is evident in this study, the phenomenon of motivation within the context of African bureaucracy involves more than an empirical process and orientation. In order to maximize performance, along with the use of motivators and hygiene described in the literature on organizations (Hertzberg, Mausner, and Snyderman 1959; Maslow 1943; and others), attention to culture and the contextual elements of the societal environment is quintessential.

Montgomery's study (1986B) concluded that the importance of motivation does not vary much from country to country; motivation is a universal concern. In the author's view, the occurrence of events in which motivation was the critical skill depicts the extent to which a significant organizational problem in African countries is the role of personal relationships in the larger institutional environment. Another problem noted had to do with the SADCC managers not being forthcoming in taking steps to improve the level of motivation. According to Montgomery, "the SADCC events showed that these managers rarely engaged in serious administrative reform efforts, even when they recognized deficiencies in the system as costs to their own and their subordinates' motivation" (24). Montgomery also wondered why top African managers so rarely displayed leadership by undertaking administrative reforms, given the fact that the African administrative systems were crying out for administrative reforms of a type considered conventional in the Western world.

A key recommendation was that in order to maximize performance, attention to culture, including the contextual elements of the local societal environment, is essential. Montgomery recommended that new approaches to leadership and the use of authority structures as part of an organizational development strategy would help managers both to identify motivational problems and to deal with them effectively. He went on to add that many of the steps required to improve motivation involve changes in the structure and mission of organizations as well as the management of individual staff.

Clearly, culture's role in administrative motivation is a partially hidden element that seemed to influence the behavior of administrators within the African context. Montgomery pointed to several deficiencies that could have benefited from some type of administrative or personnel reform efforts. He drew on the management events data to cite reported incidents that told of inflexibility in the personnel and other infrastructural support systems that affect motivation. Several examples of this in the critical incidents are: administrative delays that imposed an additional work burden on employees at the last minute; an unexpected and undesired transfer that deprived an employee of a special opportunity; and inflexibility in responding to special personnel needs. While such events provide direct evidence of how organizational weaknesses affect individual morale at lower and intermediate levels of management, no concerted effort was ever made to put reforms into place.

In his analysis of the SADCC data for this study, Montgomery determined that managers in the African context seldom act alone, suggesting that problem solving is usually not an act of individual leadership since it does not occur during conventional social exchanges. In fact, Montgomery drew on his earlier study of bureaucratic politics in Africa (1986A) to suggest that decision making does not seem to take place through the process of mobilizing a coalition to bring about the desired effect. He sums it up by arguing that reforming the system to accommodate the value preferences of individual employees may be more difficult to achieve in Africa since systemic change is not taken as a social challenge.

In "Life at the Apex: The Function of Permanent Secretaries in Nine Southern African Countries," Montgomery (1986C) examined the functions of permanent secretaries in the nine southern African countries and assessed the extent to which the political role of senior civil servants in Africa can be differentiated from their administrative roles. In addition, he assessed whether the roles and functions of African administrators were consistent with or different from those described by Henry Mintzberg (1979). This study relied on SADCC events data collected from forty permanent secretaries, their deputies or equivalents.

Among all of the nearly 1,200 reported activities and functions that were performed by these administrators, Montgomery found that environmental circumstances other than politics had the greatest influence on the activities of top African civil servants. He also found that the similarities in functions performed by administrators from the various countries were striking, given the different ideologies, colonial heritages, and traditions of the countries studied. The study found that the primary task of the top government officials in southern Africa is the management and allocation of resources. For example, there were repetitive efforts expended at economizing in the use of financial and personnel resources, including the great concern at top levels over systems maintenance and other custodial functions that collectively make up the largest element in most organizational budgets. Overall, the record of the events data showed that these high level officials had a large degree of personal involvement in even trivial details of resource management. Entries from the management events ranged from items concerning design of organizational structure and details of assignment of personnel and resources, to daily decisions allocating resources in accordance with the perceived mission of the organization.

Another area of interest raised by this study was monitoring the performance of those who acted on behalf of the organization, a very important function of permanent secretaries in African bureaucracies. This function ranged from supervision of immediate subordinates to analysis of a system of management information gathering that was intended to improve performance. According to Montgomery, "the balance between personal supervision and systems of monitoring appeared in the African case to tilt toward direct action" (215). This confirms the more general finding that African administration is more a matter of personal relations than of systems (Hyden 1983).

The study also found that in the nine southern African countries the dominant concern was over resources, not strategies. Resource constraints not only dominated the allocation function, but also constituted the principal concern of the monitoring function, of liaison with different organizations, and of the negotiations and entrepreneurial activities of permanent secretaries. Montgomery noted that it is possible that this concern is characteristic of all public sector managers at the apex, as contrasted with counterparts in private enterprise, but cautions that this distinction calls for further investigation.

Still another conclusion that resulted from the study had to do with the absence of critical incidents/management events that involved politics. As the author noted, politics was rarely mentioned during the study, in spite of the ferment in which the southern African countries were compelled to govern themselves. For example, there was only one case in which a permanent secretary attended a political rally, another in which he had to leave his office to hear an important government figure speak, and one or two that might have had minor political overtones in connection with a provincial visit. Also, a political party was mentioned only once in the diaries, elections proceedings once, and public speeches not at all. There was a briefing or two of television or press representatives, although these were just to explain official policy.

From a cultural perspective, it is fair to say that one would not expect these diaries to record any activities that might be interpreted as politically disloyal (although there was the promise of anonymity that accompanied the study). To be sure, political issues must certainly have been discussed freely during the frequent informal social interactions that took place between ministers and their top administrators. And, the fact that such discussions were not mentioned very often in the critical incidents/management events that occurred during working hours suggests that the higher service in the African context is more concerned with politics and policies as individuals than as officials. It was surprising to note that top management devoted only a minor part of their "official" time toward policy issues and matters.

By far the biggest problem or concern the author raised had to do with the "reality" that in Africa, administration is more a matter of personal relations than of systems. It was also rather problematic to find that within some of the poorest countries in the world, the primary task of top government officials is the management and allocation of organizational resources. The diary entries were rife with events involving economizing in the use of financial and personnel resources, and the concern at top levels of government in these countries was over organizational maintenance and other custodial functions, including a high degree of personal involvement in even trivial details of resource management (213).

By suggesting that environmental circumstances other than politics have the greatest influence on the activities of top civil servants, culture can be expected to play an independent role in administrative action. The influence of culture seems to be quite evident as Montgomery notes that the balance between personal supervision and systems monitoring appears in the African case to tilt toward direct action (215).

In "Probing Managerial Behavior: Image and Reality in Southern Africa," Montgomery (1987A) set out to explore the relevance and accuracy of several Western images and expectations about African management that were generally taken as accurate. First, African managers were expected to be primarily motivated by the hope of personal or tribal gain rather than to improve institutional performance. This expectation was based on the fact that in most newly independent African states, the concept of public interest was only beginning to emerge. Second, because African bureaucratic organizations were transferred by imperial colonial regimes that did not follow African local institutional traditions, concern over internal problems takes precedence over broader societal goals and purposes. The third was the assumption that African bureaucratic behavior was somewhat unrealistic because the system is thought to be laden with ideology and political fantasy. Fourth, because Westerners understand the goals and functions of the private sector better than those of the public or parastatal sectors, they correspondingly expected private sector managers to be more entrepreneurial and more efficient than their counterparts. Finally, because of the political uncertainties on the continent, African managers are expected to be unusually risk-averse, especially when it comes to adoption of institutional innovations (Montgomery 1987A).

The study drew on the SADCC data, relying on both the 1,868 critical incidents recorded at all levels in response to a standard set of questions, and the 1,187 entries taken from daily diaries distributed to permanent secretaries working in these same countries. These two independent data sources were used to probe the relevance and accuracy of the five images and expectations about African administration. In terms of analysis, the statistical technique used was the frequency distribution for descriptive data analysis. Another procedure involved the classification of a larger set of management events according to the public and national goals managers were serving at the time. Other methods used in the analysis of the data were not very clear, however. For instance, the author stated, "the management events were subjected to close scrutiny for evidences of fraud or corruption, ignorance, negligence or uncooperativeness, or lack of ability, all of which are sometimes associated with personalistic administrative systems" (13).

Overall, the findings from this study showed that managerial behavior in Africa had become more sophisticated than was predicted. One of the key findings of the study was that current development theories that call for a reliance on the private sector are not as easy to apply in Africa as they might have been in Asia at a similar period of independence. Africans, Montgomery suggested, distrust the private sector and prefer to use governmental interventions. There was not much of a difference found between the level of skills and the roles played by managers in the public and private sectors in Africa. In fact, there is not a large entrepreneurial class comparable, say, to the Chinese in Southeast Asia. Thus, the possibility of relying heavily on private, voluntary organizations or other nongovernmental agencies is not a realistic option. There is not much indigenous church-supported development activity of the kind found in Catholic Latin America or even Buddhist Thailand. As for local self-help organizations, there seems to be little evidence of such an infrastructure except for football (soccer) pools and family-related activities.

The study found that international organizations working in southern Africa, whether development banks, public agencies, or universities, would endeavor to work through governments. It reemphasized the importance of training beyond the conventions of formal education. The study noted that, as a collateral finding, there are many potentially valuable institutions already in existence. In short, there are great opportunities for inter-institutional relationships in management arts and sciences.

Another finding was that the kinds of change the administrative system needs are hardest of all to bring about. Managers must develop risk-taking attitudes, become more experimental, more outward looking, and more client oriented. Montgomery went on to add that it is possible that some donors (bi- and multi-lateral funding organizations) may be able to impose administrative as well as economic conditions to their assistance, though experiences with such approaches in earlier times suggest that subtler means of changing managerial behavior will have to be found (35).

According to Montgomery, "suffice it to note here that the greatest surprise in the goals analysis concerns the almost complete absence of episodes involving the public in any way at all" (12). In this regard, he remarked that Africans are demonstrably less public oriented than they are concerned with personal matters. In fact, fewer than half of their reports of events concerned public issues, and of these, fewer than half again were described as having a positive effect. Another problem noted repeatedly by the author was that although there were many administrative types of problems in the various bureaucracies, managers rarely engaged in serious or meaningful administrative reform efforts; although, however, the events also demonstrated that when they did, the outcomes were gratifying (29).

The author recommends that to become more innovative, African managers must become more risk taking, experimental, and more outward looking, including being more client oriented (although not much guidance was provided on making this change). The study also re-emphasized the importance of training beyond the conventions of formal education.

In "How African Managers Serve Developmental Goals," Montgomery (1987B) set out to determine how African managers serve the purported goals of developmental efforts. First, he identified a series of potential goals that managers might serve in the context of a developing country. Second, he presented a frequency count of activities directed toward the accomplishment of such goals. Finally, he contrasted those efforts with the total portfolio of reported administrative functions. This list of national goals was derived from an empirical study of managerial functions in Asia, adapted slightly to relate them to national as well as organizational or internal purposes (American Institutes of Research, 1974). In this study, the 1,868 SADCC management events were recoded to show whether they displayed either "effective" or "ineffective" behavior on the part of administrators. For example, 832 events, or 44.5% of the total number, could not be coded as having a developmental impact. Most of the uncodable events had to do with interpersonal relationships and routine items that seemed to have no special relevance to a national or organizational purpose, so they could not be coded as having any goal-oriented impact (Montgomery 1987A, 17). A cross tabulation analysis was run of the events across the national sub-goals in order to determine the extent of their managerial contribution to developmental sub-goals. It was also run to provide some sense of which managerial activities were most likely to be successful. This analysis permitted both the assessment of whether there was a managerial contribution to developmental sub-goals (by country in the SADCC region) and to distinguish among goal-related activities at different levels of management.

Part of what Montgomery found after examining the SADCC data was that the sub-goals, together with the activities undertaken by the southern African managers on their behalf in the SADCC data, do not in themselves necessarily serve major developmental purposes. The activities undertaken by the southern African administrators who took part in the study, for the most part, were intermediate and inter-sectoral rather than directly productive. He went on to argue that those activities undertaken were proximate, in the sense that they were necessary to the accomplishment of larger goals. They were also representative, since they took place in one form or another in nearly all large organizations. An important observation was that developmental activities were often related to matters of "internal organization" and it was not immediately obvious how these activities would serve the public interest.

Overall, Montgomery noted that the number of instances in which managers were found to have engaged in activities that actually did advance the national goal of development, even indirectly, was about a third of the total 1,868 incidents gathered from the sample. For instance, the frequency distribution of events across the national sub-goals reemphasized the inward-looking character of managerial behavior in Africa. Most of the effort reported in the incidents had to do with upgrading staff capabilities, introducing improved management tools, imposing greater discipline within an organization, and improving organizational structure. To Montgomery, these incidents had to do with systems maintenance, an important function in large organizations. Further, the frequency with which these types of events appeared was rather disturbing. Unfortunately, activities addressing the external environment, including citizens/clients, were not on the agenda of action, even when essentially managerial features were included in the count—like streamlining services, negotiating for additional resources, or bending rules in order to get things done.

There were some significant conclusions that resulted from this study. Key among these was that there is an intense internal preoccupation by the African public officials who are charged with the implementation of development activities (and this was a negative finding). In fact, Montgomery seems to suggest that, on balance, the efforts of all organizations whose survival and growth are not directly linked to public responsiveness should be redirected toward developmental ends. The greatest surprise resulting from this study concerned the relatively infrequent appearance of episodes directly involving the public. That is, given the fact that development involves public responses, such as changes in behavior and more productive investments on the part of private citizens, it would have been reasonable to expect managers to devote some considerable amount of effort to client groups of one kind or another (358). As part of his conclusion,

Montgomery wondered whether this observed phenomenon might be responsible for the extremely slow rate of development in that part of the world. Or, as he put it, "is it overly sanguine to assume that governments see their role in development as one of generating opportunities for their citizens?" (358). Culture did not take an independent role in explaining the behavior of African administrators in this study.

In "The Strategic Environment of Public Managers in Southern Africa," Montgomery (1991) examined the extent to which African managers dealt with issues and entities in their external environment. For the purpose of this study, the external environment was defined to include relationships with both national and local political leaders; negotiations and transactions with other administrative units whose collaboration is desired for programmatic reasons; links to the administration of general or special public and informal groups. According to the author, dealing with these elements in the external environment is considered a "strategic" function of management because it requires long-term continuities of purpose and relationships. It also involves discretionary actions that may not be viewed as a formal part of an organization's mission.

Montgomery also provided a comparative basis for interpreting the southern African experience. Using frequency distribution analysis, he made it possible for the events data to be classified into all three categories of strategic management, including political, administrative and public relations. In addition to the SADCC database, Montgomery incorporated other analysis gathered over a period of a decade, on administrative experiences in Asia and Africa, as well as a small comparative sample from North America and Europe.

Two aspects of Montgomery's findings are noteworthy here for the purpose of this chapter. He observed that many newly independent countries followed the colonial pattern of administration. This involved starting the careers of the newest civil service recruits at the village level, by assigning them to either rural development or general (or district) administrative duties, then promoting them to the center (generally national capitals) later. A second finding had to do with the extent to which managers in developing countries were allowed to function in the "public" realm. As part of its conclusion, the study suggested that it is important for managers at the very beginning of their careers to prepare themselves to deal with the public, including organized subgroups, especially in situations where their work involves influencing local communities or participating in citizen groups.

A concern noted by the author had to do with administrators/ managers remaining "sensitive" to public wants and attitudes. Montgomery wondered why those engaged in developing training programs did not consider making use of indigenous experience to enhance sensitivity to public expectations. He also noted the troubling fact that managers at the higher levels of an organization are likely to be involved in negotiations with pressure groups and "special interests" rather than with the public at large, an aspect of strategic management that is ignored in most in-service training efforts. Overall, the key problems identified seemed to revolve around the inability of African administrators to adequately incorporate the external environment as part of their strategic vision, or as part of the way they do business.

Clearly, part of the strategic environment of the African administrative context involves the interplay between culture and other key factors. This is illustrated by the fact that in newly independent countries civil service recruits start their careers at the village level, often assigned to either rural development or general "district" administrative duties. In the African tradition, it is customary to post workers at the village level, so that they will first master the local setting before venturing out to the city environment. All too often it happens that when new recruits start out at the city or municipal level, they end up not understanding the dynamics of the local setting that affect the immediate public the most.

In "Differences in Administrative Characteristics Among Seven Developing Countries," Ogwo Umeh (1990) examined the extent to which six identifiable administrative skills existed in seven southern African countries, and if differences were found among these countries. The study explored the factors that might have led to these differences in addition to focusing on socioeconomic, political, and other external factors.

The findings of this study were in accordance with the contextual or ecological approach to administration. It hypothesized that the presence or absence of various administrative skills in the SADCC countries was influenced by socioeconomic, political, cultural, and other factors, operating within and from outside of the environment of a given political unit. The frequency distribution analysis performed on the data yielded some mixed results. For instance, the SADCC countries were found to differ on analytical management, organizational flexibility, and communication and public relations skills, respectively. Conversely, experiences with technical, general management, and political maneuvering skills showed much less variation. On the bivariate relationships, the amount of foreign aid per capita received by a country, the type of economic system, and the amount of foreign investment received by a country were good predictors of administrative skills.

The problems noted by the author were methodological and theoretical in nature. In the first case, the author was concerned with the need to develop more valid measures for determining what constitutes literacy rates among developing countries for comparative purposes. On the theoretical front, the author felt that there was a need for better measurement of some of the independent measures used in the study. This point was warranted because a number of the independent variables, such as rates of literacy, % of people enrolled in higher education, and type of political party system, did not lend support in the hypothesized direction.

It may be rightly said that, indeed, culture did play a role in the study. As opposed to the "universal/generic" view of administration, the study took an "ecological/contextual" view. This is a research genre that recognizes the influence of environmental factors such as the political, economic, and social conditions prevailing in a society on the functioning of public administration. To be clear, culture was not directly mentioned in terms of its impact; the ecological/contextual position taken by the study requires a sensitivity to the broader cultural context.

"Determinants of Administrative Development in Seven Southern African Countries" (Umeh 1991) explored the relationships between administrative development and the influence of environmental factors, such as the political, economic, and social fabrics of the seven SADCC countries. In particular, the study examined whether administration has "universal" status in the developed countries. This study hypothesized: H1: The higher the level of industrialization, the greater the presence of technical skills in the SADCC countries (5). H2: The higher the amount of foreign investment per capita received by a country, the greater the presence of technical skills (6). H3: The higher the amount of foreign aid per capita received by a country, the greater the presence of general management skills (7). H4: In African countries, there is a positive relationship between the type of economic system adopted and the presence of organizational flexibility skills (8).

Two types of statistical procedures were used in the analysis of the data. First, a weighted frequency distribution of the total number of management events was undertaken in order to present the management events gathered from each country as a proportion of overall management events. Then, in order to test the four hypotheses involving bivariate relationships, a cross-tabulations analysis was undertaken. The findings from the data analysis indicated that the seven countries differed significantly in the distribution of positive and negative categories of technical, general management and organizational flexibility skills. As hypothesized, the data provided support for all four hypotheses. The analysis provided a clear test of the role of socio-economic factors in determining administrative development; that is, level of industrialization, foreign investment per capita, type of economic system, and amount of foreign aid per capita, all positively influenced the presence of various administrative skills—technical, general management and organizational flexibility skills, respectively.

A problem or concern noted by the author had to do with the weak relationship witnessed in the level of industrialization and the presence of technical skills. An examination of the kinds of activities performed under the rubric of industrialization provides a partial answer to the problem. In the SADCC countries, these activities vary from country to country. In Botswana, industrial activity is limited to processing of livestock; in Malawi, it includes a variety of productive activities; in Swaziland, it is more diversified to include wood pulp, cement, confectionary, brewing, textiles, agricultural machinery, fertilizers, and color television assembly; and finally, in Zimbabwe, despite growing diversification, food processing remains the single largest branch of manufacturing and the largest employer of labor force.

Among other things, the author suggested that future studies using the critical incidents methodology should consider the factor analysis statistical technique as a useful means of identifying the range of management skills present in the management events. This recommendation was partly due to the fact that a previous study cautioned that there might be some controversy regarding the adequacy, representativeness and reliability of data gathered using the critical incidents approach (Vengroff, 1988). The role of culture was not directly explored in the study.

In "Capacity Building and Development Administration in Southern African Countries," Ogwo Umeh and Greg Andranovich (1992) examined management capacity in the SADCC countries. They developed three skill clusters for the critical incidents management events (intra-organizational relations, inter-organizational relations, and community relations). They used descriptive data analysis to classify the incidents (by country, by administrative level, and by performance outcome), and finally discussed the implications of these findings for the development of management capacity in the region.

The distribution of management skills in the SADCC region was found to be uneven, and the authors suggested that technical assistance or management training should be responsive to national and organizational differences. The data showed that middle level managers seemed to be highly represented at training sessions. The skills most often used—general management (an intra-organizational skill) and political maneuvering (an inter-organizational skill)—were also cited by high and middle level managers, indicating a similarity in managerial approaches.

While the importance of middle level managers in the African administrative context was unexpected, the similarities in the use of management skills reported by high and middle level managers are problematic for capacity building purposes. According to Umeh and Andranovich, "the categories of general management and political maneuvering skills were common at both levels of administrative responsibility, and both skills were also reported as providing net negative outcomes in managerial activities" (66). In addition, the large numbers of events at all levels of responsibility in the three main intra-organizational skills—clerical, general management and policy analysis skills—point to the narrow, internal focus of most managerial activities. The unevenness of the incidence of management events—between nations and between levels of responsibilities within nations—were noted as a major challenge for building management capacity in the SADCC nations (66).

The authors recommended that a serious and concerted effort at capacity building in Africa should assume a broad-based focus encompassing the integration of all levels of administrative responsibility. Linking high and middle level managers to avoid duplication and achieve a net positive outcome in intra-organizational management would seem a likely avenue for building management capacity. In addition, the large number of net negative outcomes in several skill clusters should be used to guide future education and training by recommending that African managers focus on the identification of common problems. That would be a first step toward managing change and development.

Although culture did not play an independent role in their analysis, Umeh and Andranovich noted, "the lack of broader external focus for development administration may be detrimental to the implementation which is often decentralized and requires broader participation than is currently evidenced in the community relations management events. This step requires a sensitivity to national culture and change, and how change affects the administration of government" (66).

In "The Conduct of Managerial Work and Its Performance in Southern African Countries," Umeh and Andranovich (2001) addressed the relationship between administrative skills and performance in the southern African countries. They undertook an exploratory examination of the use of administrative management skills and their relationship to the conduct and performance of managerial (bureaucratic) work within the context of administrative management in the SADCC countries. Although the term "relationship" suggests a two-way process—a political system influences the conduct and performance of public administration, the prevailing management capacity implicitly shapes societal policies—this study, however, focused on the former aspect.

Descriptive data analysis again provided the basis for the study. Frequency distribution analyses were run in order to obtain an ordered count of the occurrence of the various skill categories in the management events, the distribution of the conduct of managerial work by skill categories, and the distribution of performance (outcomes) of managerial work by skill categories. Overall, the study found that certain skills were in great demand in the southern African region, including organizational flexibility, communication, and adaptability/innovation skills (527). Public officials in these countries seemed to exhibit tendencies that illustrate that managing intra-organizational relations is the core activity of managerial work, with general management skills being the most noted skill cluster. The SADCC data showed that most public managers in the southern African countries seemed to focus much of their efforts on the internal workings of their agency or department, often around routine tasks and not achieving effective results. These data support Moses Kiggundu's (1989, 41-42) observation that critical operating tasks are delegated upwards in administrative hierarchy. This is a result of several possible factors: the politicization of administrative work, management style, previous experience, or internal weakness in the performance of these tasks. Another important finding was that certain skills that are needed because of the positive performance outcomes associated with their use, are quite lacking in the southern African region: organizing, communicating, and negotiating. Among the reasons for the absence of these skills are the highly volatile political, social, and economic environments that don't give public managers time to plan; weaknesses that exist in carrying out the basic operating tasks; the lack of strategic management skills; and structural weaknesses. Again, Kiggundu has described these skills as necessary for completing strategic management tasks (1989, 61; Montgomery 1991).

While the authors noted that this situation had to do with the fact that administrative management in the SADCC region seems to be inward looking, to the neglect of skills needed in strategic management activities, they did not reach out to examine whether there was a cultural basis for this. The authors recommended that institution building needs to link management education and development in public, private, and not-for-profit sectors, as this would be a tremendous aid to intensive, long-term growth efforts (66-67). Finally, they went on to suggest that capacity building for intensive growth would profit from the use of other barometers, including outreach (both local participation and resource contributions), responsiveness (meeting actual demand), and sustainability (continuity through innovation and adaptation).

Richard Vengroff's "Policy Reform and the Assessment of Management Training Needs in Africa" (1988) and "The Nature of Managerial Work in the Public Sector: An African Perspective" (Vengroff, Belhaj and Ndiaye 1991) investigated the degree to which the management roles identified in the United States can be applied generically to the public sector in the African context. Part of the study's purpose was an effort to test Henry Mintzberg's findings in non-Western settings. More specifically, the analysis of the universality or limits on the applicability of Western management roles were expanded to include managers in a Francophone African country.

Although the research methods employed were different from those used in the SADCC study, the same skill/activity categories identified by Montgomery were used for purposes of analysis in the Central African Republic (CAR). Questionnaires were administered to officials drawn from various ministries in CAR. Analysis of the data was completed in several steps. First, the distribution of responses on individual items was examined and item means were computed. Using the means, the various management activities were ranked in terms of both time and importance. In order to determine the consistency between the management activities of public sector managers in the CAR and those in other nations, a factor analysis was used to determine whether the patterns of management actions and roles in the United States identified by Mintzberg (1973) for the private sector and refined by A.W. Lau, A.R. Newman and L.A. Broedling (1980) for the public sector, were applicable in other cultural environments, particularly Francophone Africa.

In the first article, Vengroff argued that African training could be useful in two ways. First, training aims at providing reform in the area of private sector management, both for individuals who will be encouraged to leave the service through Golden Handshake and early retirement programs, and for recent and future secondary, technical school and university graduates, who can no longer be guaranteed employment in the public sector. The second goal of training is aimed at making the existing bureaucracy more efficient and better able to adapt to the changing demands associated with policy reform; this was the main focus of the analysis.

The second study found that the most important commitments of time by management level functionaries in the CAR's Ministry of Rural Development was the use of their technical skills, predominantly agriculture and veterinary. An examination of the factors and the loadings of the individual items revealed that these were reasonably consistent with those suggested by Mintzberg for the private sector and even more so with the findings of those studying public sector managers (Vengroff, Belhaj, and Ndiaye 1991, 101). Overall, the study found that to a large extent, the roles and characteristics common to public sector managers in African nations appear to be quite similar to the roles of public officials in Western developed countries.

Based on the findings of the second study, the authors suggest that these findings, along with those of John Child (1981), John Seddon (1985) and Merrick Jones (1989), imply that we must take into account the relationship between similarities and differences at the micro (behavioral) level resulting from contingent factors. They added that there may be some room for the successful application of Western management practices in African organizations. For this to work, adaptations designed to address cultural differences in behavior must be made.

Culture seemed to have played an important role in the study. The authors noted that while the roles of the United States and African countries may be similar at the macro (systems) level, the impact of the environment on the decision processes associated with those roles is significantly different. The historical factors, most notably the colonial administrative structures and practices, are still felt in the day-to-day operations of African bureaucrats. The data (and the resulting findings) are also quite consistent with Seddon's findings on the uncertainty avoidance dimension—a cultural characteristic found among African managers (107).

The authors noted that the African culture has an important impact on organizational behavior. They drew on the work of Seddon (1985) to note that the paucity of administrative resources is linked with the intense social pressure to which these individuals are subjected by kin groups. For example, the African managers place great emphasis on the importance of the social group, the collectivist side of the collectivist/individualistic dimension (108).

Finally, in "Management Events from India: A Comparative Study with African Countries," J.P. Singh's (1986) study yielded 288 management events collected in India, a number comparable to that provided by most countries in the SADCC sample. The researcher in this particular project coded only the goal-setting events. Singh's study was based on Montgomery's (1987B) work, "How African Managers Serve Developmental Goals." Montgomery provided a list of what, in his estimation, were goal-setting events that were instrumental to achieving national purposes. The twenty goal-setting events included activities that related to the following:

1. Influencing development strategies or emphases of specific investment decisions

2. Introducing a new agricultural, industrial, or commercial enterprise in the country

3. Developing a local capability for an activity formerly dependent on external resources

4. Discovering a solution of a more promising approach to a significant developmental problem

5. Stimulating more widespread adoption of a preferred practice or other desired public response

6. Introducing a new service or program

7. Raising standards of products or services provided

8. Changing rules or procedures to be more responsive to the needs of the clients

9. Avoiding disruption of service by timely action, despite difficulties or risk

10. Securing a material advantage or resource by negotiation

11. Improving or expanding dissemination programs or techniques

12. Expanding an institution's authority, status, or character

13. Developing more effective working relationships with local agencies or sources of external aid

14. Introducing the use of analytic, data-based management aids

15. Introducing cost- or time-saving measures or ideas

16. Imposing tighter structure or controls on staff or vendor performance

17. Improving the allocation or organization of responsibilities and functions

18. Upgrading the caliber, capabilities, or morale of the staff

19. Upgrading physical facilities or equipment

20. Improving record keeping or information retrieval systems (Montgomery 1987B, 237-239)

According to Singh, several of the goal categories were absent altogether from the Indian sample, and the frequency distribution among the others was slightly different from the totals in the SADCC tables. In India, the events that were coded "positive" (that is, actually serving the goals involved) were 38% of the total, as contrasted with 29% in southern Africa; and the number of events coded as not serving national goals was smaller in India. However, the study observed that the major goals served appeared in essentially the same order in both settings. One of Singh's principal findings was that "African managers seemed to be mainly concerned with organizational and bureaucratic issues," while "Indian managers were also concerned with technical and substantive issues" (33). Overall, the author notes that this conclusion is based on the higher proportion of management events in India involving technical skills, a larger proportion of positive events classified under "motivation," and a much lower proportion of events involving rules and procedures, bureaucratic politics, and interpersonal relations (33).

Next Steps

The SADCC-related studies, especially Montgomery's observations of the African preoccupation with matters of "internal organization," raise several points that need further elaboration. We close out this chapter with a critical analysis of the research. Our review of the research based on the SADCC data shows a tendency to unduly use Western administrative tools and models as the yardstick for gauging performance in these developing countries. At issue is understanding why the African administrators get so preoccupied with internal matters, and what can be done about it.

Clearly, one of the biggest impediments to development in Africa is resource constraints. As a result of constraints brought about by inadequate resources, African managers and administrators are forced, at times, to take a very pragmatic stance when it comes to bureaucratic decision-making. To the African manager, for example, it is often inconceivable to have to put so much emphasis on the external environment when, in fact, the internal aspects of the organization are completely in disarray. Although this phenomenon may not appear to be very intelligible to the Western outsider observer, in the African administrative context it is of high significance. It is quite reflective of the African cultural environment, and makes sense to those working within the African setting.

A number of factors, the most significant of which is culture, might account for the fact that African administrators appear to be "inward versus outward-looking." Milton Esman (1974) noted that the developing countries do not have the type of social, economic, administrative and political structures that the current developed countries enjoyed when they were developing. For example, the Western countries had a reasonably secure political base for modernization. Major governmental and political structures were in place, and a sense of national identity linked individuals and social groups to the political system. Within society at large there were widespread entrepreneurial and other organizational capabilities that were harnessed to perform a wide variety of developmental functions. Finally, societal demands for public services, although they appeared to be intense at the time, were modest by modern standards. Overall, the demands on the government were moderate and well within the government's capacities to handle.

To the contrary, it is clear that most of the developing countries today do not share the conditions that characterized Western countries during the period when classical administrative doctrines were formulated. In the newly developing countries, the cement of nationhood was and continues to be fragile; the structure of the state was, and still is, not firmly in place. National symbols command little support; the policy is riven by ethnic, religious, and regional cleavages; and the criteria of legitimacy for rulers and procedures for succession have not yet been institutionalized. Entrepreneurial, managerial, and professional skills are acutely in short supply, and there is little experience with indigenous voluntary organizations for modern economic and governmental purposes. Finally, demands on government for public services have been intense, far in excess of administrative or economic capabilities. For example, the claims for services covered every section of life from infrastructure—roads, power, irrigation, and telecommunication—through assistance in agriculture and industry, to demands for education, welfare, employment, and housing. These circumstances create burdens for governments in contemporary developing countries, which their Western predecessors did not have to face with the same urgency and intensity.

At the same time, in southern Africa the most dominant and durable cultural characteristics come to the forefront and provide a rationale for organizing efforts to address these demands. Thus, the African notion of collectivism, characterized by a tight social framework in which people distinguish between in-groups and out-groups and expect their in-group (relatives, clan, organizations) to look after them in exchange for a debt of absolute loyalty (Hofstede 1980) must play a more central role in the analysis of why things are not changing in Africa. Therefore, although African culture may not espouse and exhibit a "public interest attitude" openly as is the case in the West, the collectivist orientation provides a way to examine the relationship between state and society.

Much of the reality of African administrative management can be understood through a cultural lens. Two key cultural characteristics that dominate the SADCC data include issues of personalism and pressure by kin groups. For example, civil servants are said to see their functions in personal terms, and their role presumably permits them to engage in "corrupt" practices that are required by economic conditions and family relationships. This also implicates the cultural element of collectivism (Hofstede 1980; Hyden 1983; Etounga-Manguelle 2000; Seddon 1985). In fact, a close examination of events associated with bureaucratic politics, for example, demonstrated the fact that "personalism" works as a managerial style (Montgomery 1987A). The next chapter provides a more nuanced assessment of how culture reflects and influences African public administration.

Chapter Five

The Interpretive Framework and Public Administration

Public administration has essentially been characterized through the Western models of the nation-state and Western notions of development. Goran Hyden argued in *No Shortcuts to Progress*, however, that a key failure in our understanding of Africa's lack of development was the inability of Western models to come to grips with culture as an independent influence on development policy. In the case of Tanzania, culture's influence was captured in the concept "economy of affection." For Hyden, this economy of affection is composed of a network of support, communications, and interactions among structurally defined groups connected by blood, kin, community or other affinities. Consistent with this type of communal system of production, household units cooperate for both productive and reproductive purposes. Hyden pointed out that belonging to an economy of affection had implications for social change and transformation, particularly in development policy and administration, since members relied on the communal system to meet basic survival, social maintenance, and developmental needs. In this way, the economy of affection provided an alternative to state policy that had a decidedly local flavor (Hyden 1983; Friedmann 1992).

Hyden's work has continued to be a starting point for discussions of the independent role and influence of culture on state policy and administration. This chapter addresses the challenges and dilemmas posed by the economy of affection by bringing culture back into the analysis of development public administration. We begin by briefly revisiting how culture is linked to and influences African public administration. We recognize that "African culture" is an oversimplification and that many different cultures exist across sub-Saharan Africa. In the beginning, our desire to link culture as an independent influence on administrative practice, however, keeps us at this more global level of discussion. Later on, we focus on administrative practice in one specific nation, Botswana. We use Botswana because its history and relative peace and prosperity have made it stand out in the southern African region. Our focus also includes a re-examination of data collected by USAID and NASPAA to assess the management training needs in southern Africa.

Culture and Administration in Africa

Culture, as other scholars have argued, has a tremendous influence on society in general, and for our purposes here, in administrative work settings in particular. Edward Hall, for instance, concluded that culture controls our lives in many unsuspected ways (1959, 52). What is most important is that culture seems to mask more than it reveals. Thus, as an independent influence on administrative workplace performance, if culture is simply taken for granted rather than examined critically in terms of how it conditions a society's expectations of its relationship among and between different departments within government, then positive effective change will not occur. In a more general sense, the focus on culture in a comparative context helps to reveal some of the variations in public administration, including differences in administrative practices.

Howard McCurdy (1977) discussed the influence of local conditions upon the chances for administrative success, especially in the developing countries of the world. Concern with local conditions grew out of experience with technical assistance programs in Asia, Africa, and Latin America. McCurdy's account is consistent with the experiences of scholars who worked overseas under the auspices of the World Bank sponsored programs during the heyday of the Comparative Administration Group (CAG) in the 1960s. The efforts of those early comparative administration scholars helped to bring into view the importance of culture in understanding and improving the practice of public administration (Riggs 1976; Heady 1987; Jun 1976). In fact, as McCurdy states, "the ecological approach pretty well destroyed the idea that there were any universal principles of good administration that could be applied with equal force in all countries, rich or poor. It meant that professional public administrators, instead of beginning with an ideal model of administrative efficiency, had to begin with local conditions as local officials saw them and fashion administrative solutions to fit..." (McCurdy 1977, 298-299).

McCurdy documented certain administrative challenges that have been known to be endemic to all developing countries. In fact, in some respects, these complaints appear to derive from some of the cultural traits found in these developing African countries:

- Executives in developing countries are incapable of delegating authority. They want to control everything. Even the simplest administrative decision has to be approved at the top.

- Carefully written development plans just gather dust. Officials in developing countries have no interest in the actual administrative details necessary to accomplish the plans.

- Corruption is out of control. Development funds are siphoned off to hire friends or relatives. In some cases the money simply disappears.

- So much time is wasted on the forms of management paperwork, big staff meetings, field trips. But when it comes to the guts of management—communicating objectives, defining responsibilities, delineating staff and line operations—they are just hopeless.

- There is too much secrecy. The circulation of management information is severely restricted within the agency. You even need special permission to get copies of public documents.

- Nothing works. How can you run a government department when the telephones don't work and mail isn't delivered? (McCurdy 1977, 300-301).

These descriptions (or complaints) of the failures of administrative practice have dominated the Western literature on development administration, and have been touted as obstacles to effective administration in developing nations. However, upon closer examination these complaints document the problems facing African states pinched between the pressure to produce the economic benefits of prosperity, on the one hand, while promoting peace and order on the other (Sandbrook 2000). And all of this has taken place within political systems in which the founding vision was a remnant of the colonial past. Claude Ake, for example, characterizes the situation in this way:

> At independence the form and function of the state in Africa did not change much...State power remained essentially the same: immense, arbitrary, often violent, always threatening...politics remained a zero-sum game; power was sought by all means and maintained by all means. Colonial

rule left most of Africa a legacy of intense and lawless political competition amidst an ideological void and a rising tide of disenchantment with the expectation of a better life (1996, 6).

The relationship between the African state, African politics, and African society is very complex. Cultural variables thus provide important clues in the effort to better understand this complexity, and in particular the nature and practice of public administration in the African context. While the nation-state "grew" along with the economic, political, and social modernization in Western societies, this has not been the case in the Third World. Using the West as a model, however, leads to a conflation of these different sets of images resulting in a misapplication of the values inherent in the Western model to African (and other Third World) societies. Other recent literatures, from both postcolonial and African studies, on the problem of the nation-state in Africa have observed that the African state is a hybrid that emerged through a process of transculturation and cannot be easily understood from the perspective of Western modernity. At the heart of this argument is the call to examine not only the globalizing and homogenizing aspects of development but also its more regional, local, and diverse aspects.

Bringing Culture In: Theory

Culture has been defined to include many different social, political, organizational, and economic characteristics as we showed in chapter 2. In his forty-nation study, Geert Hofstede found that many of the differences in employee motivation, management styles, and organizational structures could be traced to differences in national cultures. More specifically, "when we speak of the culture of a group, a tribe, a geographical region, a national minority, or a nation, culture refers to the collective mental programming that these people have in common and is different from that of other groups, tribes, regions, etc. Hence, we are all conditioned by cultural influences at many different levels— family, social group, geographical region, and professional environment" (Hofstede 1980, 43).

Organizational culture can be thought of as the glue that holds an organization together through a sharing of patterns of meaning. In organizations, culture focuses on the values, beliefs, and expectations that members come to share (Siehl and Martin 1984, 27), the customary and traditional way of thinking and doing things (Peters 1989), rituals and ceremonies (Smircich 1983), and the pattern of shared beliefs and values that give the members of an institution meaning and provide them with the rules for behavior in their organization (Davis 1984, 1).

Shamsul Haque (1996) argues that the organizational cultures of bureaucracies in the developed nations are quite different from the bureaucratic cultures in Third World countries. Basically, he suggests that the nature of public administration in the developing countries is "contextless." That is, significant differences exist between Third World countries and Western nations in terms of the nature of the relationship between their overall administrative systems on the one hand, and their economic, political, and social contexts on the other. In Haque's view, while administrative arrangements in Third World countries reflect their exogenous origins (both colonial and post-colonial), the administrative systems in the Western capitalist nations represent their endogenous societal contexts (1996, 315-316). Overall, Haque contends that knowledge of indigenous culture is important to fully understand and appreciate the nuances of administration in a particular nation.

O.P. Dwivedi and Keith Henderson have made a similar observation. They contend that administrative policies go beyond the national bureaucratic values and are often influenced by cultural assumptions based on differences in race and ethnicity. Their point seems to be that the indigenous cultural values have an impact on the administrative systems; that the idea of value-free public administration is a myth rather than reality; and that the borrowed Western administrative models have been incompatible with and ineffective in non-Western societies holding different and unique sets of values (Dwivedi and Henderson 1990).

So how can culture be brought into the analysis of public administration in Africa? In his work, *Compatible Cultural Democracy*, Daniel Osabu-Kle argues that culture is key to positive and effective development in Africa, and that establishing culturally compatible political preconditions is different in Africa than it is in the West. This is because African politics based on a culture of cooperation and compromise and competition is seen as destructive (Osabu-Kle 2000, 74-75). Africa's rule of law, Africa's diffusion of executive power, and Africa's safeguards against the abuse of executive power—in practice these principles derive from different sources and conditions than their similar sounding Western counterparts. In fact, African communities lived by rules that, through knowledge gained by trial and error, were found to fit the particular environment in which the community resided. This knowledge usually was believed to come from the teaching of ancestors and ultimately from God; the result was the prominent place held by religions in the rule of law, which resulted in parallel systems of power during the colonial era. Responsibility and accountability to the community were tied to both religious and community authorities. However, the rules were not developed and applied in a top-down manner.

As Osabu-Kle further notes, the diffusion of executive power through power sharing, or people's participation, was integral to the success and effectiveness of self-development. He also points out that this was not the colonial experience, nor has it been the post-colonial experience where top-down authority has been the norm in African nations. Indeed, the ability to balance interests and to offset power with power (for example, religious with economic power, central with local power) was central to success. Thus, compensatory processes, or what we might call checks and balances, helped to limit the abuses of power and provided a safeguard against excessive executive authority.

These principles, like democratic principles in the West, were an ideal to be achieved, of course. However, given the insertion of the colonial state apparatus into Africa, these principles have been submerged within the regime of colonial and post-colonial power described by Ake. In this light, the general conclusion reached by Patrick Chabal and Jean-Pascal Daloz—it isn't that today's Africa can't or won't modernize, but rather that Africa works in a way that is different from Western societies, and the role of the state and the relationship between state and society is different—can be linked to their conceptualization of culture as an independent influence. Overall, even if one were to disagree with their analysis, Chabal and Daloz make a powerful case for changing our paradigm for analyzing African politics, suggesting that Africa's present circumstances encourage the creative use of "the traditional," or African values (1996, 147).

Bringing Culture In: Administrative Practice

How does culture affect administrative workplace performance? In examining the literature that exists on the issue of culture, particularly those studies that were based on the SADCC management events, there was a clear indication that culture did have a notable influence in the conduct and practice of public administration in the African context. However, it is interesting to note that in these studies culture had a unique way of directly or inadvertently serving as the factor upon which certain unexplained behaviors, occurrences, or phenomena could be understood. The four studies discussed below had the most to say about the role of culture in administrative practice, and we return to them for a closer look.

In his study, "Levels of Managerial Leadership in Southern Africa," John Montgomery (1986B) examined the relationship between managerial behavior and motivation within the African bureaucratic context. In this study, the importance of motivation was quite noticeable in the management events provided by the officials from the various SADCC countries. That function appeared in 377 situations, or 20% of the total number of events examined.

Montgomery concluded that culture had a lot to do with the observed phenomenon of low levels of motivation in the SADCC bureaucracies. According to Montgomery,

> similar problems are posed when the system itself has to be challenged in order to bring about a remedy. As might be expected, managers were much less successful in dealing with systemic problems than in addressing motivational problems on a personal basis. Some African administrative institutions are deeply rooted, though "new" as aspects of an independent political system, and they often draw upon traditions far older than even the colonial period itself. Management events revealed the existence of a complex system of ethnic arithmetic, by which tribal preferences took precedence over formal procedures for recruitment and promotion. Such behavior often appears mysterious and irrational to the outside observer, although its counterparts can be found in government operations everywhere. In the African situation, few managers were prepared to deal frontally with such issues, even if they were causing morale problems in their own staff (1986B, 21-22).

The above quotation clearly suggests that culture, including ethnic preferences, tradition, and African values, plays an extraordinary role in determining how African managers go about motivating employees in their public bureaucracies. As part of this study, Montgomery recommended that in order to maximize performance in the organizational environment, attention to culture, including the contextual elements of the local environment, is essential. In the study, "Life at the Apex: The Function of Permanent Secretaries in Nine Southern African Countries," Montgomery (1986C) concluded that environmental circumstances other than politics have the greatest influence on the activities of African top civil servants, and that culture can be expected to play an independent role in administrative action. One example that Montgomery used to demonstrate the role of culture was in the performance monitoring function of those who acted on behalf of the organization. It was a function that ranged from supervision of immediate subordinates to analysis of a system of management information gathering that was intended to improve performance. In Montgomery's estimation, the balance between supervision of subordinates and systems monitoring appears in the African case to tilt toward direct action (1986C, 215). In fact, Montgomery rightly drew on Goran Hyden to bolster the contention that African administration is more a matter of personal relations than of systems (Hyden 1983). The implication of this is that in the African context, work seems to be accomplished within the cultural milieu of the ongoing personal, kinship, nepotistic relations that dominate the environment of administration. In other words, most of the time there is great deference to the informal network of personal relations, to the neglect or avoidance of established bureaucratic frameworks and processes. In essence, it is this cultural, informal, personal network orientation, rather than the official processes, that provide guidance to managers when they engage in official administrative transactions.

In his study of "The Strategic Environment of Public Managers in Southern Africa," Montgomery examined the extent to which African managers dealt with issues and other organizations in their departments' environments. According to the author, dealing with the external environment is considered a strategic function of management because it requires long-term continuities of purpose and relationships, and because it involves discretionary actions that may not be viewed as a formal part of an organization's mission.

A key concern noted by the author had to do with public managers being "culturally sensitive" to public wants and attitudes. For example, Montgomery was concerned that those engaged in, say, developing training programs, did not consider using indigenous/cultural experience to enhance sensitivity toward meeting public expectations. Overall, Montgomery's view was that African administrators should do a better job of incorporating the local environment as part of their strategic vision, as a way of managing the public sector more effectively (Montgomery 1991).

In their study, "Capacity Building and Developing Administration in Southern African Countries," Umeh and Andranovich examined the issue of building management capacity in the SADCC countries. These authors found that the distribution of management skills in the SADCC region was uneven. They went on to suggest that technical assistance or management training would need to be responsive to national and organizational differences. Overall, although the authors did not demonstrate the effect that culture had on the performance of administrative tasks, they noted that culture added "layers of complexity to the tasks of public management." They suggested that the lack of a broader focus on the external environment for development administration may be detrimental to policy and program implementation, which is often decentralized and requires broader participation than is currently evidenced in the management of community relation skills. In sum, they suggested that this step calls for a sensitivity to national culture and its effects on administrative and institutional change (Umeh and Andranovich 1992).

Next we turn to the re-examination of management events in the country of Botswana, with the goal of identifying and then assessing how local cultural characteristics are reflected in those events.

On the Importance of Local Government

The 1998 World Development Report devotes an entire chapter to the importance of local government reform in developing countries, and a widely cited World Bank report states that an effective public sector in a modern developing country depends on the ability of the central government to harness the resources of lower levels of government (Cochrane 1983). In 1989, the World Bank and the Italian Ministry of Foreign Affairs sponsored two workshops on strengthening local government in sub-Saharan Africa. Participants included delegates from twenty African countries and observers representing numerous foreign aid donors. According to the World Bank, the strengthening of African local governments could be regarded as essential for the rehabilitation of national public finances and hence a means to sustainable growth and development (World Bank 1989, 1).

The emphasis on the reform of local governments, especially in the sub-Saharan African countries, is premised on five crucial factors. First, effective local governments are perceived as providing opportunities to involve long-neglected citizens in the decision-making process (Hyden 1989; Olowu 1989). Second, mobilization of local governments may be especially important in Africa because many countries have been severely affected by structural adjustment and required cutbacks in central government budgets. Third, local governments have the potential, given Africa's rich local institutional heritage, to help mitigate the negative effects of structural adjustment programs on the poor. In a more empowered form, local governments are likely to be in a better position than the central government to recognize the precise impact of various adjustment policies and to allocate scarce resources where they will help the most. Consequently that would mean providing the poor with better access to services and infrastructure (Olowu 1989, 1). Fourth, some analysts believe that a local government initiative will be required to tackle the challenges raised by the twin pressures of rapid population increase and urban growth in Africa during a period when the severity of these problems is declining in many other parts of the world (Cochrane 1983).

Writing on local government and national planning, Peter Koehn concluded that local governments can play a vital role in identifying the pressing needs of local residents, incorporating local priorities into the national development planning framework, and promoting and defending citizen interests at higher levels of policy review and budget allocation (Koehn 1989). Similarly, it has been argued that while central government support and coordination is certainly required, local governments must play a more active role in providing adequate public services, promoting population control, and developing a climate conducive to job generation, particularly in secondary cities and small towns where tradition plays an important role in the government-society relationship (Olowu and Smoke 1992).

It is clear from this brief review that some key elements are central in defining the role of local governments in developing countries. These factors are also some of the essential elements underlying the implementation of decentralization and democratization. Local governments have the ability to first, involve local citizens; second, mobilize citizens and resources; third, create a mechanism for empowering local citizens in allocating resources; fourth, develop a system to provide the poor with better access to services and infrastructure; and fifth, provide a climate conducive to the equitable distribution of services and resources. In all, local governments can play an invaluable role in strengthening the process of democratization in developing countries, including Botswana (Umeh 1993).

Botswana is one of the most stable countries in the developing world (Danevard 1995) and had an impressive economic growth rate in the years between 1965-1989 thanks to the discovery of diamonds in the early 1970s (World Bank 1989). The bureaucracy plays an important role in policymaking in Botswana, in part due to the nation's peaceful independence, and in part due to the lack of radical ideology that has characterized policy elsewhere in the region. Taken together, these factors have limited the interference by politicians, leaving ideology out of policymaking and day-to-day planning. As a result, Botswana's administrative capacity, for the most part, hasn't been overtaken by politically and ideologically driven considerations. In addition, Botswana offers an environment that is very supportive of local democratic governance. The country has been exceptional in its political openness, competition and adherence to law (*Africa Today* 1993). Similar language and culture is shared by about 70% of the nation's small population (Sandbrook 2000, 9). Although the nation's elites have captured a disproportionate share of Botswana's growth proceeds, it has an equally unusually high flow of resources to local governments.

As Louis Picard (1987) and William Tordoff (1988) note in the case of Botswana, local government has a long history. While Botswana is no different than any other country in Africa, the strategic choices made by the "center" avoided the kind of centralization seen in most of Africa. The battle over bureaucratic reform dates back to 1970, when the future of local government wavered between the Ministry of Finance and Development Planning (MFDP), and the Ministry of Local Government and Lands. The result was that the Tordoff Commission recommended that council staffing and finance be substantially improved. Since the adoption of the recommendations of the Tordoff Commission, local government has been a major component of Botswana's political system (Picard 1987). The Ministry of Local Government, Land and Housing (MLGLH) is the "primary" ministry over all local government in Botswana. Because it is a unitary state, local government has no constitutional status and is purely a statutory creation. Basically, MLGLH plays a key role in virtually every aspect of local government, including controlling or supervising key decisions regarding local personnel, budgeting, development planning, and self-help projects; ensuring conformity with national policies and priorities; providing training; developing new revenue sources; and developing new managerial systems and procedures. Even when local governments seek greater autonomy, their primary spokesperson and advocate (and sometimes, foe) is the MLGLH. As a result, this ministry is critical to all aspects of local governance in Botswana (Picard 1987).

Regarding local government effectiveness, the Botswana bureaucracy presents a complex and mixed picture of local personnel and institutional capacity. On the positive side, there is the presence of a functional administrative structure that is in place, generally accessible, and filled with competent personnel. Several studies validate the fact that the existing bureaucratic structure has been able to live up to its expectations; prepare and execute budgets dealing with personnel; oversee the maintenance functions of several large, complex departments; and implement other administrative activities (Peters-Berries 1995; Picard 1987; Tordoff 1988; Dahlgren 1993).

Local authorities do engage in local fiscal planning, prepare development plans with specific project proposals, and manage the implementation of a large number of capital projects on an annual basis. According to some analysts, in doing so they must, among other things, deal with slow, cumbersome bureaucratic process to obtain funds from the MFDP and balance the requirements of contractors, MLGLH, and the MFDP. As a result of all this, or perhaps because of it, local governments in Botswana have an excellent record of developing key services such as water, education, and health (Tordoff 1988; Holm 1987).

The level of resources in Botswana is higher than those found elsewhere in southern Africa, where local resources are very limited (Peters-Berries 1995). The quality of local government staff is quite impressive in terms of their "paper" qualifications and their demonstrated competence and professionalism with regard to number and type of personnel slots authorized and filled at the local level. With the exception of "industrial class" employees (primarily laborers and other unskilled personnel), all local government personnel have been hired and managed by the Unified Local Government Services (ULGS) since 1973. The recruitment of other personnel is the responsibility of local councils (Dahlgren 1993). In spite of all of this, one concern regarding personnel and administrative systems in Botswana is the breadth of coverage of qualified personnel. Other researchers have noted that less competent personnel are in place in the remote rural areas, and that many intermediate posts are vacant throughout the ULGS. Whenever these vacancies are widespread, they do weaken local governance (Dahlgren 1995).

The weakest link in the Botswana bureaucracy is financial administration (Peters-Berries 1995; Cheneaux-Repond and Kanengoni 1995). The reasons for this are that budget projections are frequently inaccurate, audits are often as much as three years behind, and funds sometimes are misallocated (for example, capital funds into recurrent expenditures). In 1989-90, only three of fourteen urban and district councils produced their final accounts on time and only two received unqualified appraisal by auditors. Other problems include minimal capacity to collect local revenues and little evidence of ability to analyze expenditure on efficiency. An example of this is the extremely poor cost-recovery system for local services. Also, estimates and actuals regarding locally collected revenues often differ by 100-200% (Briscoe 1995).

Other areas of weakness are in the realms of personnel management, management of information systems, and a lack of programmatic focus at the local level in the various sectors. For instance, local personnel do not conceptualize their areas in a strategic, problem-focused and systematic sense. This was partly due to the ongoing habit of expecting direction from the "center" and the reality of central government dominance over planning and capital investment decisions. Hence, there is usually very little strategic or programmatic initiative at the local level.

Re-interpretation of the SADCC Management Events

The SADCC study identified management training needs in the southern African region. Underlying the descriptive analysis of existing practices is the influence of culture. Because the SADCC study used, as one component of data collection, the critical incidents methodology, these original descriptions of management events can be used to identify potential cultural influences on administrative management practices.

In pursuing this line of interpretation, we are guided by the extensive information on the characteristics of culture in general, and of African culture in particular, that have been distilled from the literature. As part of these reviews, it was found that a number of cultural characteristics exist that help to define the African administrative context. We rely on the results of two sets of cultural characteristics that blend the two dimensions of culture. Geert Hofstede's multi-nation study provides the macrolevel dimensions of culture of how a society sees its social, political, economic, environmental and ecological setting. Daniel Etounga-Manguelle's recasting of structural adjustment as culture adjustment points to the important microlevel dimensions of how people experience and understand their lives at home, with friends, and in the workplace.

Hofstede came up with four dimensions for classifying national cultures: power distance, uncertainty avoidance, individualism-collectivism, and masculinity-femininity (Hofstede 1980). Another set of dimensions of cultural characteristics was suggested by Etounga-Manguelle, who identified nine cultural categories specific to Africa. These categories include:

- Hierarchical distance
- Control over uncertainty
- The tyranny of time
- Indivisible power and authority
- The community dominates the individual
- Excessive conviviality and rejection of open conflict
- Inefficient homo economicus
- The high cost of irrationalism
- The cannibalistic and totalitarian societies (Etounga-Manguelle 2000, 68-74)

These identifiable cultural elements provide the basis for the identification and re-interpretation of the management events gathered from Botswana. In reviewing these events, the "usable" critical incidents (management events that were linked to a dimension or category of culture based on the content of the critical incident narrative from those who attended the NASPAA/USAID effort) were then subjected to close re-examination. These fell into the following categories:

- Uncertainty avoidance
- Individualism-collectivism
- Masculinity-femininity
- High cost of irrationalism
- The tyranny of time
- Inefficient homo economicus

In the following subsections, each of the above-mentioned cultural categories is discussed, and the management events that are associated with them are described. Our purpose is to illustrate the clash of values that occurs, and how its interpretation can differ. On the one hand, the public servant is doing the right thing; on the other hand, this way does not always fit into the performance orientation of public service.

Uncertainty Avoidance

The uncertainty avoidance dimension indicates the extent to which a society feels threatened by uncertain and ambiguous situations, and tries to avoid these situations by providing greater career stability, establishing more formal rules, not tolerating deviant ideas and behaviors, or believing in absolute truths and the attainment of expertise (Hofstede 1980). Etounga-Manguelle refers to this as control over uncertainty; the tendency for people to accept uncertainty about the future, taking each day as it comes (2000).

The management events characterizing this cultural dimension include the following (event numbers are provided in parenthesis):

- As soon as I came here, I found that my predecessor had drawn up a training program for the staff identifying who goes where, when (#2002).

- A group of trainees sent to USA were quarreling among themselves and the matter had become a source of embarrassment to us. I sent my deputy to USA to sort the matter out and she did an excellent job by getting the aggressive member transferred to another unit (#2003).

- We froze expatriate employment due to lack of housing. One of my colleagues who needed an expatriate badly, went out to look for a house. I was very happy with his initiative and approved his hiring an expatriate (#2006).

- A colleague suggested a system for distributing seeds to farmers using cards and this has been working perfectly (#2012).

- I noticed that when things went wrong, my officers shifted the blame to other ministries but the others also blamed us for procedural failures (#2034).

- One of my subordinates drew up an annual schedule for promotion, transfers and confirmation. Later, during the year, she put up to me the list of officers to be confirmed, promoted and transferred according to the schedule (#2056).

- The District Adult Education Officers were charged with the responsibility to develop methods of reporting on the progress of their work. One of the officers came up with a well-planned set of forms, which were adopted for us by all (#2082).

- We wanted the posts of the registry clerks to be upgraded; this request was turned down because of a general rule imposed by the Ministry of Finance (#2111).

- I was recruited to the present post because I had the right type of experience. I had failed to be employed as a manager because I had not done accounts work (#2172).

- I tried to request transport for use in my department, but I did not know that the proper procedure for doing so was to send a project memorandum to my superiors (#2225).

- Once I consulted my boss because many cattle were destroying crops and I could not decide whether or not to impound the cattle. My boss said that I should not touch them because the law forbade me from impounding the beasts before three months, whereas the law actually specified that I could do that within a three-month period (#2226).

- Our personnel training officer interfered in our departments affair by transferring me without the knowledge of the head of my department or the head of the council secretary (#2230).

- I was to conduct a course at a place outside my working place. I arranged everything. As I was about to leave for the place, my boss made me cancel my trip stating that I had not briefed him earlier about the tour (#2255).

Individualism-Collectivism

Individualism-collectivism is the next category. Individualism implies a loosely knit social framework in which people are supposed to only take care of themselves and their immediate families. A tight social framework in which people distinguish between in-groups and out-groups characterizes collectivism. They expect their in-groups (relatives, clan, organizations) to look after them, and in exchange for that they feel they owe absolute loyalty to them (Hofstede, 1980). For Etounga-Manguelle, this is the subordination of the individual to the community (2000). The management events that are associated with this cultural dimension include the following:

- There has been a serious difference of opinion concerning technical education between the two ministries. The President's office called a meeting of all the concerned ministries and the matter was resolved amicably (#2007).

- Although she knew she had another assignment, my colleague failed to delegate duties to her subordinates (#2119).

- Our previous superior did neither point out our shortcomings nor did he give us any guidance. This lowered our morale considerably (#2147).

- While going through a case, a colleague of mine decided in favor of one party without providing the other an opportunity to defend as required by law (#2168).

- One of my supervisors found me not reporting for duty because I was sick, but he did not report the matter to higher ups (#2204).

- My colleagues and I worked together to solve a problem (#2235).

- My colleagues gave me some ideas about supervision (#2236).

Masculinity-Femininity

The masculinity-femininity cultural dimension expresses the extent to which the dominant values in society are "masculine," which include assertiveness, the acquisition of money and things, and not caring for others, the quality of life, or people. Hofstede found that within nearly all societies, men scored higher in terms of the value's presence than its absence even though the society as a whole might veer toward the "feminine" pole (1980, 45-46). The management events that are associated with this cultural dimension are:

- We had to close down some unprofitable mines and there was unrest among the workers. We organized a team to negotiate with workers (#2040).

- A subordinate showed no remorse when I reprimanded her about the low general quality of her work (#2109).

- When I was appointed to a new job, my new supervisor was unable to show me how to do my job, so I gathered relevant books to guide me and made a success of it (#2120).

- My subordinate drew a training program for a workshop, contacted resource persons, arranged the training equipment and made the workshop a great success. This was particularly gratifying because, before she underwent a training program in CPM, she could not do anything without being pushed (#2139).

High Cost of Irrationalism

The dimension of the high cost of irrationalism is the tendency to rely on magic and witchcraft as both a means of social coercion, and as a political instrument. This category might also include the adoption/use of unexplainable criteria by individuals as a basis to justify one's actions when faced with a situation (Etounga-Manguelle 2000). The management events that are associated with this cultural category include the following:

- Once a colleague was entrusted with a task he found difficult to perform. He therefore went and told someone else that the work was entrusted to him (the latter). When the boss came to know this, he reprimanded him for dishonesty (#2059).

- My colleague, who was not familiar with public service regulations promised his subordinate a promotion, and recommended the same to the Director of Personnel. The latter enquired whether there was a vacancy. As there was none, the promotion could not be given (#2060).

- Recently, my supervisor called me to his office and made false allegations against me to cover up his own mistakes. The top boss was away at the time (#2062).

Tyranny of Time

The tyranny of time reflects the idea of seeing space and time as a single entity; that is, there is very little concern for proactive or future planning while there is over concern by individuals to maintain the status quo or the present (Etounga-Manguelle 2000). The critical incidents associated with this cultural dimension include the following:

- My typist took a whole day to type a ten page speech written by me for my minister. Because of the delay I could not get the speech in time to my minister (#2005).

- When I was employed as a section manager, my supervisor did not confirm me in time. Out of disappointment, I resigned my post (#2173).

- The typist failed to type the drought activities report in time for the Council meeting (#2207).

- The registry clerk did not post notices advertising impounded matimela on time, so we received complaints about the delay. When asked about the reason for the delay, the registry clerk said that she was busy, but with a staff of two assistants and three messengers, she could have easily posted the notice in time (#2231).

Inefficient Homo Economicus

The dimension of inefficient homo economicus is the tendency of the African to attribute very little importance to the financial and economic aspects of life. For the African, the value of man is measured bythe "is" and not by the "has," resulting in living in the present. The management events representing this cultural dimension are the following:

- The headmaster of one of my schools spent the whole year's allocation within six months (#2030).

- When I was on leave, my subordinate overspent money and kept an unnecessary amount of spare parts in stock (#2175).

- One of my subordinates discovered a long outstanding amount owed to the Council by one of the suppliers (#2176).

These incidents, taken together, point to the difficulty in assessing administrative performance in the African context. Each of the various dimensions of culture previously described illuminates another aspect of African culture that is not immediately obvious when a different value orientation is applied to assess, for example, administrative performance. In the next section, we turn to an examination of these findings through an interpretive and cultural lens.

Discussion

One of the key challenges we are faced with in this study is to give culture a more central place in the analysis of African administrative systems. We argue that the critical facet of interpretive approaches in the field of public administration is the focus on administrative processes and how these link organizations to particular societies. Also, since administrative effectiveness ultimately is rooted in the dominant values of the local culture, multiple models and practices within the cultural context of specific nations may be required (Joseph 1998; Putnam 1983).

To what extent can the interpretive approach help in adding value to the findings of the SADCC-based management events studies? An application of the interpretive approach means more than knowing about the factually-based findings that resulted from the SADCC management event-based studies. Just as we have argued in the previous chapter, administrative effectiveness ultimately is rooted in the dominant values of the local culture, meaning these values must be taken into account when identifying how we will assess administrative performance. According to an interpretive orientation (as opposed to the logical-positivistic view), it is the tacit dimension of administrative practice that becomes important. The understanding of how culture, language, symbols, and objects are interpreted in and through administrative action is crucial. A key argument of the interpretive mode is that human actions and motivations are not only conditioned by external demands, but also are the result of an individual's interpretations of the meanings attached to external elements such as organizational tasks, hierarchical relations, functions, roles, and so forth.

So far, this chapter has shown that a view of public administration from the unique perspective of African culture provides a more nuanced understanding of bureaucratic action. As part of our closing discussion, we revisit the unique management events data collected from the SADCC countries to make some final observations on the usefulness of the interpretive approach to better understand development public administration. Although the management events data were collected as part of an effort to explore training needs in the southern African region, we contend that this methodology can also provide a means of examining the role of culture as an influence on administrative management. In fact, part of our argument in this chapter has been that the interpretive approach can greatly improve our ability and understanding of the traditionally conceptualized management events data, both in terms of being able to decipher the cultural elements implicated in those events, and then examine how those cultural components might influence performance.

Table 5.1 and Table 5.2 provide some insights into the range of administrative skills that resulted from the SADCC management event data, including the extent of their performance (for example, whether they yielded positive or negative outcomes when assessed in terms of their performance in the southern African bureaucracies). How does the reliance on an interpretive approach enhance or further our ability to provide a nuanced explanation of the SADCC management events data based on these findings?

Table 5.1 shows a preponderance of the management events clustered around the clerical, general management, and policy analysis skills, resulting in the conclusion that public managers in the southern African countries exhibit an inward, departmental focus when it comes to administration. Furthermore, public managers in these countries seemed to exhibit tendencies suggesting that managing intra-organizational relations is the core activity of managerial work. For example, in all the countries, general management was the most noted skill cluster.

In terms of the performance outcomes of managerial work and the skill clusters (see Table 5.2) the results were mixed. We suggested that policy analysis skills, although used less often, potentially were more useful in

Table 5.1

Distribution of Management Events by Nation and Managerial Skill Clusters (N = 1709)

Skill Clusters	Botswana	Other SADC Countries	Row Totals
Clerical (n = 332)	48	284	332
(Row %)	(25)	(19)	(100%)
General Management (n =523)	42	481	523
(Row %)	(22)	(32)	(100)
Policy Analysis (n = 290)	30	260	290
(Row %)	(16)	(17)	(100)
Adaptation (n = 62)	15	47	62
(Row %)	(8)	(3)	(100)
Political Maneuvering (n = 320)	37	283	320
(Row %)	(18)	(19)	(100)
Community Relations (n = 182)	18	164	182
(Row %)	(9)	(11)	(100)
Column Totals	190	1519	1709

Table 5.2

Performance (outcomes) of Managerial Work
by Skill Categories (N = 1709)

Skill Cluster	Number	Positive Performance		Negative Performance	
		Botswana	Other SADC Countries	Botswana	Other SADC Countries
Clerical	332	25 (28%)	141 (18%)	23 (25%)	143 (20%)
General Management	523	24 (25%)	207 (27%)	18 (19%)	254 (35%)
Policy Analysis	290	15 (15%)	154 (20%)	15 (16%)	106 (15%)
Adaptation	62	11 (11%)	32 (4%)	4 (4%)	15 (2%)
Political Maneuvering	320	14 (14%)	137 (18%)	23 (25%)	146 (20%)
Community Relations	182	8 (8%)	98 (13%)	10 (11%)	66 (9%)
Column Totals	**1709**	**97**	**769**	**93**	**730**

fostering intensive growth by linking the various channels through which regime policies are implemented. In addition, using policy analysis skills did contribute to effective management practice more frequently than not.

The more we examined the findings of the SADCC management events, the more interesting the findings became. Inter-organizational management, or managing and steering the department through the organizational maze that makes up the public sector in most of these countries, and an important component of intensive development strategies, was a distant second to the conduct of intra-organizational relations. In part, this may reflect how the data were coded; nonetheless, it does point up a major gap in skills needed for intensive growth. And, regardless of country, the SADCC public managers' responses demonstrated a stronger preference for political maneuvering than adaptation (see Table 5.1); this trend was particularly pronounced in Swaziland and Lesotho, respectively. In both political maneuvering and adaptation skills, the performance outcomes across these countries were mixed to negative (that is, the skills used did not contribute to effective management; Table 5.2).

Then, community relations, an integral component of intensive growth and currently an important focal point of World Bank and other donor efforts, was woefully lacking in all the countries (Table 5.1; Rondinelli 1983; Caiden 1991). Like adaptation skills, however, the use of community relations skills (community relations, communications, and public relations) generally resulted in effective management practices (Table 5.2).

While the findings presented above seem to portray southern African managers as being overly concerned with the internal aspects of the organization, it was our contention that an interpretive framework might yield additional insights from the SADCC data that were not captured or anticipated in the initial analysis. As Edward Hall (1959) suggests, because of the cultural undertones embedded in the management events, there are more meanings hidden in such data that may not have been readily apparent even to the impartial observer.

As can be discerned from the foregoing discussion, the African managers seemed to have been concerned more with intra-organizational (inward-looking) issues than the inter-organizational and community relations events. For the African manager, there seems to be more of a preoccupation with skills related to clerical duties, general management, and policy analysis as opposed to adaptation, political maneuvering, and communication skills, as was captured in the SADCC data. To the casual observer, this finding may be seen to be very troubling because it is not consistent with a Western orientation and interpretation. To the African observer, it may be an overstatement of the applicability of the Western model in the African context.

An interpretive (cultural) view of the management events data might lead us to two different conclusions. First, at a broad societal level, the events suggest that in the African context intra-organizational skills seem to be very well suited to the kinds of activities and chores the African managers engage in and their citizens expect at this phase of their development. If this is so, from an interpretive/cultural perspective, the real question should be how to help African managers and their citizens change their expectations of just what constitutes effective administrative performance, and if warranted from this examination, how to de-couple and then re-couple expectations for the government-society relationship as well as the practices of development administration. However, as the pace of globalization quickens in the region, the experiences of people, and how these experiences are mediated, will play an important role in any changes.

In a study of the determinants of administrative development in these African countries, for example, Ogwo Umeh (1991) found a weak relationship between the level of industrialization and the presence of technical skills. Part of the explanation for the weak relationship had to do with what gets counted as industrial activities. In Botswana, industrial activity largely is limited to processing of livestock; in Malawi, manufacturing and industrial sectors are dominated by foreign capital and include a variety of productive activities; in Swaziland, industrial activities include processing of wood pulp, cement, confectionary, brewing, textiles, agricultural machinery, fertilizers, and color television assembly; and in Zimbabwe, industrial activities are dominated by food processing efforts. The range and diversity of individual activities that do not place heavy emphasis on the use of specialized technical applications, contrary to what obtains in the West, leading to vastly different personal experiences with technology and its effect on everyday life. So, rather than accepting the fact that the hypothesis yielded a weak relationship, based solely on the criteria of levels of both statistical and substantive significance, respectively, which are empirical and logical-positivistic configurations, a closer look into how industrial activities are organized and what these involve, and the broader expectations of the relationship between (in this instance, economic) institutions and society is needed. The interpretive lens brings culture into play as a way to better inform analysis and practice. A focus on culture can help make the linkages between institutions and processes more transparent, even if the explanations are not entirely clear.

Implications of the Interpretive Approach Toward Cultural Understanding

By allowing us to explore and discover meanings that may not be readily apparent, the interpretive approach has far reaching implications for public administration. When we think of the administrator in a Third World bureaucracy, there is some degree of ambivalence associated with the conduct of professional duties. For example, much of the administrative framework in use in the Third World countries emerged in a Western cultural context. However, as scholars have noted, administrators in the developing countries are not totally immune from the influence of local contexts and, as a result, those administrators often encounter conflict between the formal or expected administrative behavior based on Western bureaucratic norms and local expectations of the day-to-day demands of the job (Haque 1996; Riggs 1964). It is only through an interpretive lens that such ritualism, discrepancy, or formalism can be identified. Perhaps remedial action can be undertaken to make needed adaptations.

The interpretive approach provides an opportunity to more fruit-fully articulate some of the nuances embedded in the cultural dimen-sions that have been noted to capture administrative behaviors in the African context. Two of Geert Hofstede's (1980) dimensions of national culture include power distance, or hierarchical distance, and masculin-ity-femininity. While these dimensions tend to portray much of African society to be characterized as a vertical or male-dominated society, it leaves out some necessary details. It is only by engaging the interpretive methodology that we are able to gain a deeper sense of the essential components of these dimensions. For example, through the interpretive mode we begin to discern that most human relationships in Africa are based on a person's hierarchical position, status, educational back-ground, seniority, and gender, but the effect of this is not the same as in the West. It is this hidden dimension that helps one to fully inter-nalize the two dimensions mentioned above. In addition, we also come to understand that in much of Africa, most public servants, no matter what their organizational status is, must recognize the existence of senior-junior relationships (one of the authors of this study had first-hand experience of these cultural characteristics; he worked for about seven years in one of the federal bureaucracies in one of the African countries). In fact, in the African administrative context, it will not be uncommon to find that two individuals (senior and junior cadres) maintain a highly paternalistic and trusting relationship simply because they both, for instance, attended the same educational institu-tion, or were colleagues in some capacity prior to joining the organiza-tion where they both now work.

With respect to the individualistic-collectivist cultural dimension, the foregoing relationship between a senior and junior colleague of the same educational, occupational, or social connections may not only influence one's behavior at work, but helps to broaden one's network of relationships when one seeks advice or political support. Because a senior-junior relationship is a two-way relationship, one who chooses to violate this basic norm is likely to be poorly regarded by others, and may experience diminished respect, which in turn could jeopardize future dealings with superiors and friends who may have attended the same institution. In sum, this kind of collectivist orientation has a very important effect on stability in the bureaucracy, and may even con-tribute to the inward orientation seen in the SADCC studies.

Chapter Six

Bringing Culture Back Into the Mix
Some Reflections

In a world where nothing is solid and everything is changing, it is tempting to follow familiar paths toward well-known solutions, regardless of how the nature and scope of the problems have changed. This response is itself a "prisoner of culture" if we follow a standard definition that culture is the system of values, symbols, and shared meanings of a group including the embodiment of these values, symbols, and meanings into material objects and ritualized practices. The same is true in the developing countries where the role and impact of culture is integral to an understanding of the ways of life and the processes involved on the political, social, economic, and administrative fronts. This chapter provides an explicit link between the adoption of a culturally-sensitive focus for viewing organizations and a deeper understanding of the dynamics of public administration in southern African bureaucracies. It discusses how developing countries can take advantage of a culturally-based approach to enhance other dimensions of growth, such as globalization, economic development, democratization, and decentralization. We conclude with a brief discussion of the relevance of the cultural approach for an ongoing assessment of development public administration.

The overriding theme that dominates much of our effort in this book has been to highlight the absence of a culturally sensitive orientation in the conceptualization and analysis of key dimensions of administrative management. Further, this gap presents serious limitations that undermine the application of research and evaluation findings within and across countries. The nature of our inquiry began with a critical assessment of prevailing models and frameworks used to explain the dynamics of public administration from a comparative perspective.

As part of the context of the book, the first five chapters were devoted to laying the groundwork for a culturally sensitive view of the study of administration. The first chapter described the conditions in Africa today, surveyed the literature that tried to account for these conditions, and then provided the outline of the rationale for using an interpretive perspective in understanding development administration. Chapter 2 provided a more detailed overview of the basic concepts from the comparative and development public administrative literature. Also explored were some critical dimensions of administration, along with a discussion of some of the deficiencies or limitations of past comparative public administration orientations. The chapter concluded with an identification of six sometimes competing values that underpin administrative efficacy: capacity building, participation decentralization, responsiveness and accountability, and equity.

Chapter 3 presented an exploratory mapping of the use of culture as an analytical tool for examining development public administration. In conducting the mapping exercise, the literature was used as a basis for identifying the elements of local culture that should be taken into account when considering public sector performance, including a depiction of how these elements of local culture impact performance. The chapter concluded with our critical assessment of one of the first uses of culture in the analysis of African affairs, Hyden's concept of "economy of affection."

Chapter 4 was devoted to a re-assessment of the most comprehensive study of public administration and management in southern Africa, a project conducted by the United States Agency for International Development (USAID) and the National Association of Schools of Public Affairs and Administration (NASPAA). The study involved the then-nine nations of the Southern African Development Coordinating Conference (SADCC): Angola, Botswana, Lesotho, Malawi, Mozambique, Swaziland, Tanzania, Zambia, and Zimbabwe. This USAID/NASPAA study focused on management events collected from public officials in the nine countries. We re-examined the premises established and the conclusions drawn in each of those studies, with an eye toward seeing the extent to which "culture" entered into the research design or was considered in explaining the findings. Some of the key points included an important barrier to change that needs a more explicit role in future analysis: the African notion of collectivism, characterized by a tight social framework in which people distinguish between in-groups and out-groups while expecting their in-group (relatives, clan, organizations) to look after them in exchange for a debt of absolute loyalty. Two key cultural characteristics that dominate the SADCC data had to do with issues of personalism and pressure by kin groups, two factors that underpinned much intra-organizational activity.

Finally, in chapter 5 we linked culture, as an independent influence, to administrative practice. We focused first on incidences of the different characteristics in administrative practice, relying on the SADCC critical incidents management data. Then, after examining aggregate data from the nine countries, we explored the administrative practice in one nation, Botswana, because its history and relative peace and prosperity have made it stand out in the southern African region. Once again, this brings us to the issue of methodology.

On the Problem of Methodology

The field of comparative and development public administration has continued to exhibit serious inherent problems. One is the absence of an overarching theory. Part of the challenge is overcoming the confused nature of the concept of "development administration"; that is, it is not conceptualized in any precise and generally accepted fashion. According to scholars in the field, the term "development administration" identifies a loosely-sensed interest, which exists because of people who deem it important. Its significance does not depend upon a paradigm, or a systematic array of theoretical knowledge (Siffin 2001, 6). Part of the difficulty with the field of development administration is that the guiding principles usually originate in the West, and these principles become problematic when applied to non-Western nations.

Recent examinations in the field seem to support these contentions. Ferrel Heady has noted that scholars have been unable to agree on a paradigm or a consensus as to how "scientific" their studies could claim to be (Heady 1998, 3). Heady has raised a number of other theoretical questions. What is the acceptable optimal framework for the comparative study of national systems of public administration? What are the current and prospective possibilities for achieving scientific knowledge about improvement in administrative capabilities in various settings? What are the major trends and prospects in less developed nations? How can a competent civil service operating in an inadequate administrative structure be achieved in international organizations, given the context of a global nation-state system? What are the implications for comparative and international administration of possible future system transformations (Heady 1989, 503)?

Clearly, the development of comparative and international administration was, to a great extent, influenced by Western ideas. Hence, the development of theory in the field in the 1960s and 1970s has been a reflection of the application of Western models. A common weakness among these models is that they all advocate a reliance on Western values to explain and predict administrative practice. Unfortunately, the theoretical assumptions of the Western models have been challenged quite extensively, including where the unique historical and cultural experiences of indigenous people were involved.

More recent critiques of the field of comparative administration continue to identify the preoccupation with irrelevant models and frameworks as problematic. According to Jong Jun, for example, to understand new international transformations we need to transcend the conceptual orientations of rationalism, positivism, scientific research, and macro-theory because they cannot reflect changes that occur. By shifting our perspective to ways of understanding local conditions and social interactions, we should be able to develop deeper sensitivity to the potential for global, national, and local changes (Jun 2003). We believe that the cultural approach permits this.

Globalization and Culture

Globalization, either the promising or the threatening version, is reorganizing how people deal with their everyday lives, including how the whole range of societal institutions interact (Sassen 1996). Whether at the level of language, business practices, popular activities, or the practice of religious beliefs (Berger 1997), evidence of globalization is tied to the idea of a "wired world." Globalization, however, should be thought of as the increased interconnections or interdependencies of a variety of sectors of the economy, politics, and societies so that events "there" have important consequences that are felt "here;" the exact nature of the consequences, however, is an empirically open question (Giddens 1990). This awareness of the effects of interdependence makes globalization special, but also problematic.

Culture, or the elements that create something local as "local," is an integral part of globalization and is both a cause and a reflection of growing interconnections, most of which are still being examined and remain poorly understood. Udo Zander (2002) shows how the deeply embedded values of modernity that couple capitalism, democracy, and individualism in fact have fairly complex effects on global interconnections. While the recently published *Many Globalizations* (Berger and Huntington 2002) points to the importance of local culture as a mediating force in the globalization process, there continues to be a heated debate about the factors affecting globalization and its consequences. One of the targets of this debate is the urbanization of the earth, to use Jorge Arango's (1970) phrase. As a cultural phenomenon, urbanization is a sign of economic wealth and cultural maturity (Gottdiener and Lagopoulos, 1986), terms often used to also describe development. But the downside, recognized and expressed by sociologists as the difference between the traditionally-based linkages in gemeinschaft culture and the instrumentally-based linkages in gesellschaft culture, is that cities give rise to tremendous inequalities based on the lack of close ties with other people. This is an important and understudied mediating factor in the process of developing local responses to globalization.

One of the programs that have been undertaken by the United Nations in recent times is the Culture in the Neighborhood (CIN) Project. This approach was triggered by the fact that the impact of globalization on cities appears to have been varied, producing differential effects. As a result, the United Nations has encouraged projects that address the dynamics of culturally-diverse neighborhoods in a modern urban environment. Among other things, these projects place an emphasis on social integration and participation at the local level. Basically, CIN consists of cultural activities which the residents of a neighborhood carry out through their own efforts. These activities, based on local culture, are then used as a means of fostering dialogue and interaction between "Africa" and "Europe" (UNESCO 2001).

According to the coordinators of this unique program, Culture in the Neighborhood seeks to increase mutual understanding between people of different cultures and ethnic groups. It also strives to improve the quality of everyday life for the inhabitants through the organization of concrete cultural activities in their neighborhood. The CIN project is composed of pilot projects in cities in participating African countries (Burkina Faso, Cameroon and Mozambique) as well as in European countries (Finland, France and Switzerland; UNESCO 2001).

Economic Development and Culture

There is an abundance of scholarly work arguing that culture has a role in the course of economic development. According to Michael Todaro, there are several qualities, and in a classic work on economic development in the Third World, he concluded that development is a multidimensional process involving major changes in social structures, popular attitudes and national institutions as well as the acceleration of economic growth, the reduction of inequality and the eradication of absolute poverty (Todaro 1977, 62). There are other studies (Odhiambo 2002; Valdes and Stoller 2002; Singer 2000; Leonard 1991) that view culture as having an integral role in the course of development.

The role of culture in human affairs has gained increasing attention recently. With the end of the Cold War, Samuel Huntington (1993) has argued that future international conflicts in global affairs will be determined by the cultural divide between Western civilization and the rest of the world (Lal 1998). The role of culture in economic affairs was first argued by the German social scientist, Max Weber.

In *The Protestant Ethic and the Spirit of Capitalism*, Weber (1904-1905) argued that Protestantism promoted the rise of the spirit of modern capitalism because it extolled hard work, thrift and frugality as moral virtues. Hard work and the pursuit of money are virtuous and people could organize their everyday lives to attain these virtues. Weber contrasted this to the traditional spirit in which extant everyday life was acceptable, and changes to it were resented and resisted. According to Weber, Protestantism did this by defining and sanctioning everyday behavior that was not conducive to business success (Landes 1998, 175).

In *The Wealth and Poverty of Nations*, David Landes (1998) demonstrated that the Protestant ethic worked its wonders not just in the Western world, but also in Asia. Landes characterized Japan as a society whose culture has a sense of collective obligation. This Japanese version of the Protestant ethic sets it apart from the culture of individualism in the West. Landes suggests that along with government initiatives and a collective commitment to modernization, this work ethic and Japanese personal values made possible the so-called Japanese miracle (Landes 1998, 291).

A different cultural characteristic, respect, is attributed to being the force behind economic development and achievement in other Asian countries. For example, among the newly industrialized countries of

Taiwan, Hong Kong and Singapore, a new group of Confucians contend that a culture of respect for family, hard work, and the social order is equivalent to the Protestant ethic that Weber postulated as being responsible for the rise of capitalism in Northern Europe (Allen 1998, 80).

The impact of Islamic culture on economic development in the history of the Middle East is well documented by Deepak Lal (1998). Under the Abbasid rule (A.D. 632-715), an economic miracle was achieved by unifying the countries of the Near and Middle East through Islamization and Arabization, thereby stimulating intense industrial and commercial activities (Ashtor 1976). While the Islamic culture has been marked by a history of success and failure, Lal contends that it is not Islamic beliefs in themselves that have hindered development but dysfunctional state apparatus and economic policy. When that was reversed in the Muslim parts of Southeast Asia, a period of "Promethean intense growth" was delivered (Lal 1998, 6).

While the economic benefits of a cultural investment can be difficult to measure, a 1999 "Culture Counts" conference organized by the World Bank found evidence to support the contention that there is a link between cultural investments and economic growth. In her article, "Culture Works: Cultural Resources as Economic Development Tools," Molly Singer (2000) suggests that cultural resources are major tools for building safe, clean, and smart communities. In her view, a cultural orientation is useful as local government managers and administrators create sustainable and working communities where citizens are engaging in social issues, participating in economic development, and planning their own futures.

What does cultural resource investment encompass? In Singer's view, this includes historic sites, cultural and ethnic groups, faith-based organizations, and neighborhoods. They are important resources because they help to improve communities, generate economic opportunities, and address social concerns. When properly coordinated, they can become an important part of a city or community's identity, economic vitality and social well-being (Singer 2000, 1-2).

Modernization theorists from Karl Marx to Daniel Bell have argued that economic development brings pervasive cultural changes. However, others, from Max Weber to Samuel Huntington, have claimed that cultural values are an enduring and autonomous influence on society. Ronald Inglehart and Wayne Baker tested the thesis that economic development is linked with systemic change in basic values. Data from their study were drawn from three waves of the World Values Surveys, which covers sixty-five societies and 75% of the world's population. They found evidence of both mass cultural change and the persistence of distinctive cultural traditions. Economic development, for instance, is associated with shifts away from absolute norms and values toward values that are increasingly rational, tolerant, trusting, and participatory. Cultural change, on the other hand, was found to be path dependent. For instance, the broad cultural heritage of a society, whether Protestant, Roman Catholic, Orthodox, Confucian, or Communist, leaves an imprint on values that endure despite economic development or modernization (Inglehart and Baker 2000, 33).

Others have argued along the same line as Weber. In a study examining the impact of culture and economic development in eighty Native American tribes, the authors found that cultural factors do not influence the economic conditions of a tribe, but they do influence how income is distributed among the communities (Pickering and Mushinski 2001, 20).

In the case of India, culture has helped rather than hurt the state of economic development. Castes act as interest associations in the course of the country's democracy. India's labor force has become increasingly skilled and differentiated (Riggs 1964). From the Green Revolution onward, India's farmers have consistently raised yields to meet food needs; large firms governed within joint families have succeeded in both the domestic and global arenas. Taken together, the case of India suggests that societal culture can have a positive influence on economic development (Adams 2002, 150).

In the African case, a round-table discussion on the theme Culture and Development, organized under the Ethiopian Economic Association (EEA) and attended by government officials, scholars and development practitioners, focused on the need to upgrade cultural performances to bring about a sustainable economic development. Professor Mesfin Woldermariam stressed the need to change some of the existing cultural activities that seriously affect a country's effort at economic development. In particular, he pointed out that some traditional and religious practices evident in society have a tendency to negatively affect economic development. Furthermore, attempts to strengthen societal creativity are severely affected by the fact that particular religious activities call for many more working days off, resulting in a clash of cultures over religion.

Arguing that the connection between development and culture is complex, UNECA economist Dr. Alemayehu Seyoum suggests that while society's existing culture impacts economic development, the process of development can also affect culture, making it difficult to posit a generalizable relationship between culture and economic development. He concluded by suggesting that it is necessary to think of both culture and development as part of the means of development (Africa News Service 2002).

Democratization and Culture

Of the several factors that are known to influence the endurance of democratic institutions in poor countries, cultural beliefs seem to be quite significant. In a recent study of the determinants of lasting democracy in developing countries, important variables were found to include former status as a British colony, island status, the share of the population professing Islam, the share of the population that is of European descent, penetration of the English language during British colonial rule, and a measure of ethnic homogeneity. According to authors of this study, the evidence suggests that cultural beliefs and institutional inheritances are important determinants of the viability of democracy in poor countries, even when controlling for literacy and socioeconomic development (Cleague, Gleason and Knack 2001, 14).

In their seminal study, *The Civic Culture*, Gabriel Almond and Sidney Verba (1963) contended that institutions and patterns of action in a political system must be congruent with the political culture of that society. Several studies have also attempted to identify the cultural requisites of democracy (Almond and Verba 1963; Almond 1996; Verba 1965; Baker, Dalton and Hildebrandt 1981; McDonogh et al. 1995; Weil 1989).

In the literature on democracy, three types of culture studies are most notable. The first is the civic culture theory of Almond and Verba, which is by far the most influential research in this field. In a cross-national study involving five democratic societies, they concluded that a nation's political culture has an independent influence on social and political behavior. According to these authors, culture sets the norms for behavior that members of society acknowledge and follow, even if they personally do not share these norms. The second type is Harry Eckstein's authority culture theory (1966). Eckstein's work, for the most part, discusses the dynamic aspects of culture and culture's role in processes of political change (Eckstein 1988, 1990). A third distinct version of political culture analysis was developed by Aaron Wildavsky. He drew on Mary Douglas' grid-group approach to create a typology of cultures based on four distinct life styles. He based these types on social relations and the values they exemplified (Wildavsky 1987).

In an essay on the "Culture Debate on Africa," John Ayoade examines the role of culture in democratization and nation-building. When democracy is broadly construed as part of nation-building, culture can then be seen as a social process and a part of the infrastructure which facilitates development (1989). Others argue that culture has to play a prominent role in nation-building because the biggest challenge faced by newly independent states is how to evolve a single nation from the multiplicity of ethnic groups (Toure 1969). Nation-building can be strengthened by the establishment of a cultural policy that seeks to build on the essential commonalities of culture to produce an integrative national culture. In this view, the emphasis on these commonalities reduces the differences in a multi-ethnic society, thereby furthering and enhancing the cause of democracy and nation-building.

New states in sub-Saharan Africa faced the challenge not only of building the institutional apparatus of the state, but of simultaneously constructing a national identity among disparate cultural groups. Oftentimes, these states did not establish sufficient institutional bases, such as effective political parties and efficient state bureaucracies, to successfully coordinate the mobilized interests of their populations. In such poorly institutionalized states, culture is often the primary criterion for political association, which again, is one of the key requirements for a viable democracy (Henderson 1998, 10).

Decentralization and Culture

There is no question that in African countries, cultural beliefs and practices influence the functioning of programs of decentralization. Decentralization has been viewed both as a policy and as a method or mechanism for more efficiently implementing policy. It has serious implications for a wide range of policy areas, from agriculture to health and public works. Furthermore, it is closely linked to broader efforts to improve the quality of governance and thus make policy implementation both more effective and responsive to democratically expressed needs and objectives (Vengroff and Umeh 1997, 41).

Findings on the impact of decentralization in developing countries have been quite mixed. Much of the inconsistency can be attributed to the fact that the correlation between a formally-announced program of decentralization and successful implementation is quite low, or in some cases nonexistent. While numerous countries have undertaken so-called decentralization programs, these primarily involve deconcentration and delegation rather than devolution, and few have demonstrated the political will necessary for successful implementation (Conyers 1983; Rondinelli, Nellis, and Cheema 1984; Vengroff and Johnston 1987).

In an important comparative study on the assessment of decentralization program studies in the African countries of Nigeria, Senegal and Tunisia, Richard Vengroff and Ogwo Umeh contended that the relative quality of decentralization in any country can be judged as a function of three factors: scope, intensity, and commitment. Of particular importance to us in this study is the idea of scope.

Scope refers to the breadth or coverage of the program of decentralization. Does a program have truly national implications or is it highly localized and limited in its intended application? Scope in Vengroff and Umeh's research was measured in terms of geographic coverage (does the program of decentralization apply to the entire territory of the country in a geographic sense or is its application limited to a particular region, city, type of city, or zone?) and population (are all the people in the nation considered to be involved in the decentralization program or is it limited to specific groups? Is there room for popular participation by all of the adult population or only for some particular subset thereof?).

We argue in this chapter that these measures of the scope of decentralization reflect the culture of the people for whom the program is being implemented. To the extent that the scope (in this case, coverage of the program of decentralization) is relatively broad, then chances are good that the broader values (culture) of the region, locality, nation, will lend support toward a program of decentralization. That is, a program of decentralization will have a greater chance of success if various societal values (as represented by a society's different populations) are represented and involved as part of a decentralization program effort (Vengroff and Umeh 1997).

Culture and Assessing Development Public Administration

Using a culturally sensitive framework for examining comparative and development public administration permits the analyst and/or practitioner to see behind surface appearances. In terms of development public administration, the cultural lens means cutting through three layers: development, public, and administration. If one believes that culture has an important mediating influence on how the models of public administration are applied, then the ideas that stem from our culturally-oriented knowledge bases become critical.

Academically oriented works on comparative and development public administration generally take one of three views toward the role of administration in developing countries: the extent of development isn't important to administration; the extent of development is important and is understood within the Western model of development; if the country isn't an industrialized nation, then public administration must be reconceptualized within the context of development. Our argument has been that the most often used framework is one of the first two, and our task has been to show that using a culturally sensitive, or interpretive approach can pay greater dividends for those studying, providing management training for, and working in the public sectors of developing countries. Incorporation of culture—factors such as kinship, community, time, and the lack of concern for economy in personal affairs—into sub-Saharan African public administration is long overdue. Western analysts must make it a priority for the early twenty-first century.

Chapter Seven

Epilogue
Post-Apartheid South Africa

The transition from apartheid rule in South Africa has been anything but smooth. Among the difficult legacies is the social and cultural palimpsest, overwritten by colonial, apartheid and now post-apartheid politics. The transformation of South Africa began with the decision to dismantle the apartheid state and ultimately hold democratic elections, which occurred four years later. During this period and following the elections in 1994, the idea of change was a focal point in all areas of everyday life. Daryl Glaser (2003, 218-220) notes that despite the over-politicization of South African society where mass action, intense loyalties, and undisciplined violence were a routine part of the struggle to overcome apartheid in the decade before 1994, there are now elements of shared cultural practice in the nation that can provide the basis for developing a new civil society. He points to four possible unifiers: the English language as the accepted medium for communication; Christianity; Western-style consumerism; and international sporting competitions. Whether these arenas can facilitate the development of a civil society where the peaceful negotiation of political differences can be settled and the state is held accountable to the people is yet to be seen. What role will local culture play in mediating the practice of each potential unifier? In the development of the new South Africa, these four arenas suggest where interests may converge or diverge, and who the important players might be. However, it is crucial to remember that given the long history of racial oppression in the economic, political and social arenas, the unification of South Africa will certainly take much longer than ten years (at this writing) of transformation.

The African National Congress (ANC) has dominated the political landscape since 1994, effectively mobilizing its political support around cultural symbols. During this time, the government has faced increasingly complicated and difficult policy decisions at the intersection of urban transformation, rural development, economic growth and the broader distribution of wealth, and health issues dominated by the spread of HIV-AIDS (Alexander 2003). Popular support for the ANC has remained at a high level, demonstrated by the electoral success of its candidates, even though the government's record in dealing with these issues has been mixed at best. Our examination of culture, development and public administration in Africa concludes with this brief epilogue on the new South Africa, specifically focused on how bringing culture into the analysis provides a nuanced picture of how and why development is proceeding as it has. Given the wealth of published research on this nation, we have selected several distinctive issues that we believe identify both the traditional topics as well as the edges of the envelope of development research. After a description of the organization of South African government, we will examine the role change agents played in establishing the parameters of a post-1994 state, the ANC's Reconstruction and Development Program, the Ncholo Report on administrative reform, and conclude with lessons from South Africa's bid to host the 2004 Olympic games. In each instance, we highlight the role of culture in our analysis.

New South African Government

Under the apartheid regime, South Africa was a segregated society administered by a fragmented state. A multiplicity of institutions was required to maintain segregated public services. After the 1948 election, this fragmentation worsened under the effects of more narrowly constructed apartheid legislation and the growing imperatives of racial classification and residential segregation. As Anthony Butler (2004, 98) put it, "'High apartheid' took state fragmentation to new extremes, creating supposedly independent sovereign states for each ethnic group. Those classified as Colored or Indian under this system were accorded specific rights of residence, employment, and access to public services, so necessitating an elaborate bureaucratic nightmare of 'own affairs' departments in every sector."

South Africa is a representative democracy, electing representatives at the national, provincial, and local levels. The 1996 Constitution created two legislative bodies, a Parliament at the national level (the National Assembly) and a Council at the provincial level (National

Council of Provinces [NCOP]). Furthermore, the electoral system is based on a common national voters' roll and the results should ensure proportional representation. At the national level, the Parliament members were elected using a highly proportional party list system, in which each party created a closed and rank-ordered national and provincial list of candidates. Elections are held every five years. The National Assembly's 400 members are divided into two equal groups; 200 are elected from national lists and 200 on the basis of provincial lists. Each province receives provincial list members in proportion to its population. The National Assembly then elects the President, who is the head of the executive branch of government and who is responsible for governing in conjunction with the Cabinet, which he appoints (Butler 2004, 105; Lodge 2003, 173-175).

The South African Constitution provides for three types of powers—legislative, executive, and judicial—and distributes these to each branch of government, resulting in what Butler calls "executive dominance in a unitary state" (Butler 2004, 92). The interim Constitution of 1993 was designed to guide South Africa through the transition to democracy, yet the conditions in the country made the negotiations for the 1996 Constitution difficult. As Butler notes, South Africa now subscribes to the doctrine of constitutionalism, which specifies that citizens and public officials are subject to the rules outlined in the Constitution; nobody is above the rule of law (86). The South African Constitution, in Section 2, characterizes itself as "the supreme law of the Republic;" that is, all actions, individuals, and bodies are subject to its authority (87).

Following the idea of a separation of powers to limit the concentration of political power, each of the three powers of government is assigned to one branch of government at the national level: the Parliament, the President and Cabinet, and the courts. While the President shares some legislative powers in assenting to laws and promulgating regulations, and some judicial power in the ability to issue pardons, there are also mechanisms that place the President's office under the influence of the other branches of government as well. The President is elected by the National Assembly, not directly by the people. The President can be impeached by a two-thirds vote of the National Assembly, or can receive a vote of no confidence by the majority of the Parliament, which then would trigger a general election (Butler 2004, 89).

The Constitution also mandates a number of independent offices, which are designated to protect against illegal actions or abuses of power. These include an Auditor-General, a Public Protector, a Human Rights Commission, a Commission for Gender Equality, a National Language Board, and an Independent Electoral Commission. The performance of these bodies has been uneven, in part because of funding limitations and in part because most appointees are senior members of the ANC who critics suggest cannot maintain sufficient distance or objectivity when it comes to policy failures (Butler 2004, 89; Lodge 2003, 151-152).

The executive branch dominates the South African government. It is responsible for executing the laws of Parliament, but the political executives, the President, the Cabinet, and the senior public service, run the government. Butler (2004, 93) argues that the scope and scale of governmental activities in South Africa are so complex and interrelated that certain actors are involved in the majority of significant policy initiatives in the country as a whole. The state's core includes the Cabinet, the Presidency (which includes a policy coordination unit, a secretariat, and a committee system), the Directors General (key senior public servants in each department), the Treasury, and the intelligence and security services (93-94).

The South African Constitution places the Cabinet near the top of the system of executive authority. Cabinet ministers give political direction to a million public servants and are appointed by the President. There are twenty-nine governmental departments designed to govern by ensuring that all relevant parties are informed of, and contribute to, policy decisions that affect their area of responsibility. In addition, the executive branch has the responsibility for international agreements and institutions. In South Africa's case, dealing with environmental treaties, World Trade Organization regulations, the Southern African Development Community (SADC), the African Union, and the New Partnership for Africa's Development, are but a few of the major responsibilities.

At the apex of executive power is the President, who serves as the head of the party, head of the state, and head of government. The President appoints ministers and directors general, chairs the Cabinet and determines how it will operate, chairs some Cabinet committees and appoints the chairs of others, and shapes international policy. The President can dominate policy by virtue of these broad powers. He also appoints a large number of public body members, providing extensive political patronage positions. In close liaison with the Government Communications and Information Service, the President is the center of media attention. From this vantage point, the President's powers seem endless, and including reducing the significance of the full Cabinet, threatening ministers with dismissal, and using outside advisers to second guess the ministers while denying them any real opportunity to clarify their positions. The President also can alternatively use coordinating or dispute resolution procedures in the Treasury or within the ANC to override opposition (Butler 2004, 94-95).

The Parliament has two chambers, and legislation must pass through both the National Assembly and the National Council of Provinces (NCOP). The legislature's most important duties, outside of representing the people, are approval of the budget and its portfolio committees that oversee the activities of the various government departments. Since the establishment of Parliament in 1994, a number of steps have been taken to make it more accessible and more accountable, as well as motivate and facilitate public participation in the legislative process. One of these steps included launching a website, which encourages comments and feedback from the citizens.

The National Assembly's 400 members are presided over by a Speaker. Its function is to represent the people and to ensure democratic governance as required by the Constitution. The National Assembly elects the President, provides a national forum for public consideration of issues by passing legislation, and scrutinizes and oversees executive action. In the 1999 national election, the African National Congress (ANC) gained 266 seats in the National Assembly; the Democratic Party, 38; the Inkatha Freedom Party, 34; the New National Party, 28; the United Democratic Movement, 14; the African Christian Democratic Party, 6; the Pan Africanist Congress, 3; the United Christian Democratic Party, 3; the Vryheidsfront/Freedom Front, 3; the Freedom Alliance, 2; the Afrikaner Eenheidsbeweging, 1; the Azanian People's Organization, 1; and the Minority Front, 1 (Burger 2002, 1).

The National Council of Provinces (NCOP) consists of fifty-four permanent members and thirty-six special delegates. It represents provincial interests at the national level. Delegations from each province consist of ten representatives. Before it can make certain decisions, the NCOP needs a mandate from the provinces. It cannot, however, initiate any bills concerning money. That is the sole prerogative of the Minister of Finance. The NCOP also has a website which links Parliament to the provincial legislatures and local government associations. NCOP Online provides an opportunity for viewing draft legislation and allowing the public to make electronic submissions. A bill passed by the National Assembly must be referred to the NCOP for consideration. A bill affecting the provinces may be introduced in the

NCOP. After the Council has passed it, the bill must be referred to the Assembly. A bill concerning monetary issues must be introduced in the Assembly and must be referred to the Council for consideration and approval after being passed. If the Council rejects a bill or passes it subject to amendments, the Assembly must reconsider the bill and pass it again with or without amendments. By August 2002, 730 bills had been passed since 1994 (Burger 2002, 2).

The new South African government has also undertaken an intensive effort to modernize its public service. The public service has been consolidated since the first term with the goal of strengthening the management echelon. At the heart of this public service modernization effort is the Batho Pele (People First) initiative, which aims to enhance the quality and accessibility of government services by improving efficiency and accountability to the recipients of public goods and services. To extend Batho Pele into electronic government, the Gateway Initiative was launched to provide information on all government services through a single Internet portal.

Other modernization initiatives included negotiations on the transformation and restructuring of the public service; a review of macro-benefits (housing, medical aid and pension); the development of a competency framework and competency-based recruitment and performance management system for the Senior Management Service (SMS); the development of the Public Service Human Resource Development Strategy; the development and implementation of an Action Plan to alleviate the impact of HIV/AIDS on the public service; and the implementation of the Public Service Anti-Corruption Strategy (Burger 2002, 1).

Overall, national departments in South Africa cover the range of activities one would expect in any modern state. These include spending departments in health, housing, defense, and education, external affairs, foreign affairs, defense and intelligence; security and justice, (including intelligence, safety and security, correctional development); and home affairs. In addition, there are economic departments: of trade and industry, labor, and minerals and energy. Other departments are concerned with intergovernmental relations and public sector reform. The key department, however, is the Treasury, which incorporates finance ministry and public expenditure control functions, and has launched an ambitious new financial management infrastructure for the public service (Butler 2004).

In his book, *An Ordinary Country: Issues in the Transition from Apartheid to Democracy in South Africa*, Neville Alexander describes the peculiarities of the transition to democracy in South Africa. In Alexander's view, some unique elements are peculiar to the history of a country that, taken together, account for the continuities and the discontinuities between the old apartheid regime and the new democratic institutions. These factors include (1) the role of external circumstances; (2) the role of African National Congress (ANC); (3) the role of minority white regime; and (4) the role of certain individuals, or what Alexander refers to as the "Madiba factor" (Alexander 2003, 44).

The Role of External Circumstances

Alexander suggests that it was the overt and covert internal struggles of the oppressed people of South Africa against the economic and social deprivations of the system of racial capitalism coupled with international sanctions and diplomatic isolation which pushed the apartheid strategy of the ruling group up against its ceilings and forced big business to contemplate alternatives to the regimes of John Vorster and P.W. Botha (Alexander 2003, 44-45).

The Role of the African National Congress (ANC)

Among other things, the African National Congress (ANC) is considered part of the "miracle" of South African transition from a dictatorial to a liberal democratic state. The author states that the ANC, like all similar ethnically- and racially-based organizations before the Second World War, did not question the international legality of the South African state. Rather, they rejected the legitimacy of the white minority and white supremacist governments that ruled the territory between 1910 and 1993 on the grounds that they had not been elected by all the eligible citizens (Alexander 2003, 46-49).

The Role of the Minority White Regime

In this instance, Neville Alexander argues that the racist ideology adopted by the political representatives of the white minority in South Africa as part of negotiation with African National Congress (ANC) leadership, detracted from their ability to maintain their stronghold on power, vis-à-vis that of the ANC. In the author's words,

> The unconstructed racism of a Vorster and a P.W. Botha led to a situation where the leadership of the white minority made their move (across the Rubicon) too late to enable them to retain effective political power. Their real mistake was that they had misread the willingness and ability of the ANC leadership

to accept the neo-liberal orthodoxy. To their, and most others' surprise, they found that their leverage vanished in front of their eyes as the real ANC stood up to be counted, as opposed to the mythologized communist and terrorist organization which they had dressed it up as for the benefit of their various local and international constituencies for these decades. This misjudgment on the part of the leaders of the National Party after the ignominious departure of Botha from the scene explains the subsequent precipitous decline of that party (Alexander 2003, 49).

The Madiba Factor

The Madiba Factor, the author suggests, was, and still is, extremely important in the South African transition. More specifically, he points out that the South African style, which characterized the negotiation process, the oscillation between genteel and brutal interventions, the transparency and the secrecy of the transition, was to a large extent the result of projections of the key players: Mandela, Mbeki, Ramaphosa, Buthulezi, De Klerk, Kobie Coetzee, Pik Botha, Constand Viljoen, and Roelf Meyer (Alexander 2003, 53).

Tom Lodge asks whether the new South African government represents a new bureaucratic class in the making, and responds: "I do not think so" (2003, 31). His reasons illustrate the complexities inherent in replacing the old culture with a new one, and the clash of values that make any transformation a long-term process. These include the continuities with the old South African government. The new South Africa is still working with a colonized public service and all of the warts (waste, corruption, and mismanagement) associated with this (Lodge 2003, 129-152). Structurally, the downward push of political authority from the national level shifts the problems of policy administration to the sub-national levels (Agranoff et al. 2000). The continuing egalitarian traditions that informed the ANC's revolutionary consciousness, supported by the continuing strong role of organized labor in the country's politics, will play a part in facilitating or inhibiting this transformation as well. But what role?

The contrasting positions of those who support Western ideas that politics should be located in an active civil society, and those who support African ideas that African communities should be where politics are located, are both viable. However, given the prominent role of the international economy in South Africa, and the fact that the South African national government has become more removed from the economy as it has embraced the values of privatization and decentralization, coupled with the lack of institutional resources available to most civic associations operating at the local levels (Zuern, 2000, 124-132) and the lack of clarity regarding the roles of traditional leaders at the local level during the transition period (Ramutsindela, 2001, pp. 74-85), illustrate the importance of culture in analyzing how the transformation to a new South Africa might unfold.

Change Agents

In general, three types of change agents have been evident in South Africa: international organizations, bilateral Western donors, and internal efforts within the country (Bornstein 2000; Cumming 2001; Filatova 2000; Hyden and Mukandala 1999). Underlying the idea of effective change is shifting the terrain of politics. How each aspect of the transformation of South Africa is defined, leads to the choice of means available to policymakers to address needs. The meanings of "development," "democratization," and "reform" are contested, both in the abstract sense of theories of the transition and in the real sense of economic versus the broader measures of human development. The nature of the criteria used to determine democratization is changing, too (Koelble 1999). Whose interests are served by change? In his critical analysis of the transition to democracy, Ian Taylor differentiates between the forms democracy can take. He is not sanguine about the role change agents played early in the transition. Taylor's analysis begins by pointing out that as an opposition movement, the ANC's politics and its supporters focused on resistance against apartheid (Glaser 2001, 161-199). In the debate surrounding the end of the apartheid regime, the ANC's position was supportive of socioeconomic redistribution and the accountability of political leaders to the people. What happened instead was that a neo-liberal form of democracy emerged, based on limited popular participation, the privatization of state-controlled sectors and reliance on the market to provide for the general welfare. Taylor explains this policy shift by linking the politics of power to the politics of support in the transition, and shows how culture influenced this shift in the ANC's position. One of the keys to the eventual democratic process that emerged was the convergence of several interests, including established political elites, domestic and transnational corporate interests and aspiring elites in the ANC (Taylor 2002, 38).

As the different groups within the ANC positioned themselves to define the ANC's role in the transformation of South Africa, the

Africanists embraced the idea of Black capitalism and the rise to economic and political power of a new middle class. This vision, and the position that it articulated, quickly became one that resonated with the existing economic and societal structures in South Africa; South Africa established a policy of Black Economic Empowerment that called for corporations to sell off parts of their businesses, on favorable terms because of the legacy of apartheid, to Black businessmen (http://www.bmfonline.co.za./bee.htm). In fact, several of the political rivals of President Mbeki left politics and pursued business opportunities after he became President. For example, former Gauteng Provincial Premier Tokyo Sexwale was profiled on the American television news program *60 Minutes* on April 26, 2004, in a segment called "Comrade Capitalist." *60 Minutes* showed the rise of Tokyo Sexwale, from his Soweto roots, training in the former Soviet Union to overthrow the apartheid regime, serving time as a political prisoner on Robben Island, rallying with Nelson Mandela in the early 1990s, to his currently being known as "Deal a Minute" Sexwale, whose companies are worth over $500 million and range from minerals, banking, engineering, and health care ("Comrade Capitalist" 2004). While not all Black South Africans benefited from the Empowerment Program, aspiring political elites in the ANC were well-positioned to do so, and after he lost in the 1997 election, Sexwale turned to private life.

During the early years of the transition, the ANC received a lot of advice and assistance in a hearts-and-minds campaign that ultimately established the boundaries for debating the new directions for South Africa. Ian Taylor's example of the potency with which the change industry operated during these times is IDASA (now known as the Institute for Democracy in South Africa; formerly, it was the Institute for a Democratic Alternative South Africa). IDASA was formed in 1987 by Frederik van Zyl Slabbert and Alex Boraine, members of the corporate-funded Progressive Federal Party (Taylor 2002, 42). In the end-of-apartheid White politics, this party represented "the compassionate face of liberalism" and the interests of big business in South Africa. In IDASA's early days, it promoted dialogue between groups with opposing viewpoints and then shifted to promote what Taylor describes as "essentially a neo-liberal viewpoint" (43). IDASA was receiving funding from and co-sponsoring events such as conferences and seminars with the American embassy, USAID, the National Endowment for Democracy, British Petroleum South Africa, the European Union, the Ford Foundation, the Johannesburg Chamber of Industries, the Rockefeller Foundation, Shell South Africa, Unilever, SA Breweries, and the Standard Bank Foundation, among others (43). Most of these organizations promote democracy, voter education and good governance programs as these programs tend to help maintain a status quo view in elite policymakers and the public at large.

Indeed, the idea that an elite level consensus could be developed behind closed doors to resolve many of the challenges facing the new South Africa may have informed some of IDASA's backers (43). In practice, Taylor points to the objectives of the National Endowment for Democracy (45): first, to identify and support an emergent Black middle class; second, to develop a network of politically moderate Black community leaders, and; third, to encourage alliances between the Black middle class and White business leaders. IDASA took the message to opinion leaders and other supporting organizations to bolster public opinion and make it easier for the ANC to shift its position from socioeconomic redistribution and political accountability toward a more limited agenda for democracy.

Whether out of domestic fears (for example, civil war), international exigencies (for example, economic growth in a global economy), or some combination of these factors, the ANC embraced the existing economic relations of South Africa without the political trappings of apartheid. In so doing, the ANC also accepted the global market rather than the oppressed people in South Africa as its lighthouse during the transition period. In this way, the culture of domination and control that existed under apartheid remains in the background of the major economic and political institutions of the new nation. By giving the global economy a major role in focusing the institutional arrangements for the transition, South Africa faces the same future as the other nations in sub-Saharan Africa: while the Africanist tradition played a catalytic role in revolutionary politics, it has been relegated to a secondary role in the evolutionary politics of the new South Africa.

The Reconstruction and Development Program

If the ANC's political position shifted by the mid-1990s, then it should come as no surprise that any development program would reflect these new politics. The Reconstruction and Development Program (RDP) was the first off the blocks in 1994, and it reflected the revolutionary values of trade unionism and the liberation movement, particularly COSATU (Congress of South African Trade Unions). A broad political consensus, however, concerned the importance of the RDP to right past wrongs (Koelble 1999, 106; Turok 1995). Its short shelf life and demise in 1996 in favor of an alternative, GEAR (Growth,

Employment And Redistribution) shows how important culture is to the understanding of public administration.

The RDP's goals were simple: to alleviate poverty and to reconstruct the economy. RDP took an empowerment approach to development, suggesting that the people affected by government projects ought to participate in project planning. Furthermore, projects ought to focus on increasing national investment in manufacturing, job creation and insuring basic needs while providing access to all segments of society, and should include private sector contributions (Lodge 2003, 55). Yet the implementation of these goals was fraught with difficulty (Turok 1995). According to COSATU and the South African Communist Party, for example, the RDP was a "decisive break" with the past (Lodge 2003, 56) and was premised on redistribution, economic reconstruction following a path of "inward development," the government's role as the coordinator, and people centered and people driven development. At the same time, the government's 1994 RDP White Paper took a more measured tone even though it too called for a smaller government and more privatization (Lodge 2003, 56). The RDP's goals were premised on the idea that without growth, there would be no development; this, in turn, would undercut the possibility of a structural transformation of society. The government's role was conceived as an "enabler," following the trend captured in the World Bank's Development Report of 1997.

Evaluations of the RDP depend on one's politics. Supporters point to the achievements of the effort, including better living conditions, improved services, and better life chances (Lodge 2003, 57-67). The benefits from RDP include 12,300 new lunch programs established in schools, 550 health clinics constructed and 2,400 more upgraded, and the implementation of pregnant women and children under age six receiving free health care. In addition, 1.75 million more households have electricity, 1,500 schools have been renovated, and 1.1 million new low-income housing units were constructed, with over 1 million new water connections and 1.8 million telephone connections established (Lodge 2003, 57-58). However, this is not to say that the promises of universal health care, a social welfare system and free education are readily available. Critics of the RDP suggest that its real function has been to bring together business, labor, civic associations, and agricultural interests under the banner of bettering South African society; the RDP is merely a symbolic gesture toward nation-building, rather than a practical path for alleviating poverty and transforming society (Koelble 1999, 112-113).

Furthermore, the quick rise of GEAR as a replacement strategy for the RDP gave many the impression that the government was backtracking on its promises. (GEAR was moved under a different ministry in 1996 and a new minister, a former head of COSATU, was appointed after the election; Lodge 2003, 26.) GEAR was founded because of fear that low-level economic growth would affect the government's ability to provide services, coupled with a volatile year in the South African financial market (Mokate 2000; Koelble 1999, 114). Unlike the RDP, however, GEAR adopted market-based measures to enhance economic growth. The question remains, however, how did it get adopted so fast? Explanations vary, and many critics blame the undue influence of foreign investment capital and the tendency in the West to "right size" government operations (Lodge 2003; Koelble 1999; Mokate 2000; Turok 1995). However, it is important to remember that the leadership in the ANC was shifting and had embraced black entrepreneurship; GEAR was consistent with this shift.

The RDP represented a program grounded in revolutionary and liberation values of redistribution and participation. Its demise and replacement by a market-based program that limited the government's role reflects the contradiction between Western and African values in the context of a global economy. Anthony Butler (2004, 138) points out that the "Washington consensus...[around] trade liberalization, market deregulation, and fiscal conservatism" has been unrelenting during the last few decades of the 20th century, and influences South Africa's leaders today. Because this "consensus" holds such sway, the debate between Africanist and Western paths to development is less ideological and based more on pragmatic concerns today. That the South African government is using affirmative action and Black economic empowerment both to create a Black middle class and reduce racial inequality in the distribution of wealth indicate that the government is addressing the most significant concern of citizens—unemployment (Butler 2004, 141-143). Unlike many of the other nations in the region, South Africa's rebellion against apartheid wasn't simply against the institutions of indirect rule, it was "anti-ethnic, political, unionized, and ideological" (Butler 2004, 140). Still, the shambles that were the reorganized South African public service during the tenure of the RDP negatively affected the program's implementation performance (Turok 1995, 317).

The Ncholo Report

If the RDP represented clashing values (that is, between redistribution and governmental efficiency) and therefore was on shaky ground to start, then the deals made to "convert" the South African public administration from its apartheid institutions to its post-apartheid form would be critical to the nation's transition. Indeed, these deals effectively shifted the conflicts in South African society into the machinery of government, and helped to diminish the potential of the RDP. In 1997, the Ncholo Commission, which reviewed the South African public service, issued a scathing report on the condition of public administration in the new South Africa.

The reorganization of the South African public service is best characterized by the description "continuity" (Turok 1995; Lodge 2003; Butler 2004). First, all of the public servants in the nation retained their positions, thereby burdening the new government with the capacity challenges of the old. Second, the old apartheid system of administering by race/ethnicity continued (Glaser 2001, 92-108). Third, the new governmental structure required enhanced coordination between the different levels of government, particularly the provinces and the central government, and a more urgent need at the local level (Butler 2004, 101). The "failure" of the RDP and the adoption of efficiency and deracialization as the criteria for further reorganization has illuminated a number of challenges facing the new South African public service administration. These were captured in the *Provincial Review Report*, presented in 1997 by the Ncholo Commission (Crase and Dollery 1999).

The Ncholo Report, requested by the Minister for the Public Service and Administration, examined "leadership and strategic management, the linkage between national and provincial departments, how financial and other resources are managed, and the management of people" (Crase and Dollery 1999, 10). The commission included a team of fifteen specialists in public administration who met with nearly 1,000 public servants from all the provinces. Lin Crase and Brian Dollery concluded that "the reader is left with the overwhelming impression that state incapacity in South Africa is largely due to a lack of administrative skill in the public sector" (1999, 11).

Lisa Bornstein's (2000) review of the institutional context of the new South Africa identifies some of these challenges. While Gauteng and the Western Cape provinces were generally well-managed, the other seven had a variety of administrative and managerial problems, including inadequate financial management (three provinces were near financial collapse), information utilization, and several human resource management problems (from shortages of skilled staff to wide-ranging fraud and theft). Furthermore, the legislation did not mandate development planning across provinces, adding further stress and confusion to the administrative side of government. While it is easy enough to look at the old apartheid administrative structure as a cause for this situation, the causes for and location of South Africa's administrative incapacity are complex and historical.

The idea that simply following the World Bank's proposed path (first, establish education and training to build skills, and second, shift service provision to the nongovernmental sectors but pay for such services with public funds; Crase and Dollery 1999, 12) would solve these problems may have been shortsighted. However, the government's first step was published in a 1997 White paper on "Transforming Public Service Delivery" (the Batho Pele White paper). The document clearly spells out the "people first" (Batho Pele) principles that were to be applied to national and provincial departments: consulting users of services; setting service standards; increasing access; ensuring courtesy; providing more and better information; increasing openness and transparency; providing redress; and getting the best value for money. Although couched in the Sesotho language, the principles are similar to those espoused by the "reinventing government" movement (Osborne and Gaebler 1992). Furthermore, the existing gaps in public service capacity were evident in the implementation of the Batho Pele approach; in its 2000 compliance review, the Public Service Commission found that the South African public service had not yet remedied the problems underlying the demise of the RDP. Among its six findings (Public Service Commission 2000, 115-120) were a "general lack of practical skills in the public service to apply the Batho Pele principles," the fact that service improvement was seen as separate from the day-to-day operations of departments, and that the principles had not yet changed the daily administrative routines. The Commission also found that the costs of service improvements were not built into the operations of service providers, did not link unit performance to individual performance, and frequently consisted of lists of consultants or organizational procedures rather than actionable items.

Addressing these gaps is a large order, and the 1998 White paper on "Public Service Training and Education" established the South African Management Development Institute (SAMDI) to begin doing this. SAMDI has developed a program focused on areas identified as urgently needed, providing both functional workshops and process workshops existing in concert with European nations. Examples of the functional workshops offered by SAMDI to provincial governments and national departments in 2003-04 were: assessor training, asset management, community development, ethics and anti-corruption training, financial management, various human relations management topics, management principles, mentoring, policy management, provisioning, report writing, and service delivery (training data provided by B. Bernard, Manager, Office of the Director-General, SAMDI, personal communication 7 June 2004). There were also training workshops in advanced management development, change management, communication strategies, gender equity, management and leadership skills, managing HIV-AIDS, performance management, policy development and implementation, project management, and the senior manager's seminar. In addition, SAMDI sponsors process workshops on such topics as Batho Pele implementation for middle managers, strategic management, team building, excellent customer care, and conflict resolution.

However, if the central and provincial administrative services are at least considered by these measures, the same can't be said for local governments, where the plight is more pressing and where citizens, communities, and government come together. The 1994 Constitution establishes three categories of local government: unicities (the six largest cities in the nation are considered Category A and have metropolitan councils), the newly created districts (forty-seven districts that cover mostly rural areas are considered Category C), and the 231 smaller towns are considered Category B (these are often located with Category C districts; Butler 2004, 101-102). Most of these cities are facing severe resource limitations and administrative capacity challenges surrounding fiscal management and service delivery. Behind these general considerations, land reform, housing, health care, and crime form the policy challenges facing South Africa's cities (Seekings 2000). In addition, for the largest cities, the effects of and responses to globalization have led to debates over whether any of these cities can become "world class" cities, competing with other major metropolitan areas around the world for investment, jobs, and status.

Bidding for the Olympic Games

International sports events have become the cultural currency of the times (Roche 2000; Burbank, Andranovich, and Heying 2001), and South Africa's important May 2004 victory in the competition to host the 2010 Soccer World Cup signals the challenges and opportunities facing all developing nations. The euphoria over the $3 billion-plus financial benefit and the projected 160,000 jobs that hosting the World Cup will bring over the next six years is surpassed by the prospect of forging a new South African identity after struggling through ten years of post-apartheid democracy. All of this will be played out on the world stage as unrelenting international media exposure will place South Africa in the consciousness of every person with a television set, radio, newspaper, or internet access leading up to the

Cup competition. In the midst of South Africa's persistent pursuit of international sporting events are indications of the path this nation might pursue and strategies it might adopt to realize a new identity. The failed South African bid (host city, Cape Town) to host the 2004 Olympic games provides a case study of these efforts.

Hosting international sporting events such as the World Cup and the Olympic games typically consists of four distinct phases: the bid; if selected by the International Olympic Committee (IOC), organizing the event; staging the event; and the legacy period following the event. Given the decade-long lead time preceding the staging of international sporting events, there is a potential to target resources and a fixed timetable for development programs and projects on a scale that is hard to match under ordinary conditions. The legacy period following the event also provides infinite opportunities to revisit the linkages to social and technical progress that are part of the image of the Olympic games and represent a nation's commitment to certain values consistent with a "world class" status. Oftentimes, however, the interests of financial elites, developers, and the tourist industry capture the levers of policymaking to the detriment of broader social and political goals (Burbank, Andranovich, and Heying 2001). The Cape Town 2004 bid, however, represented a departure from this model.

The primary innovation in the Cape Town bid was the addition of human development to the three elements required by the IOC (the sports event, a cultural festival, and environmental awareness). Human development to the local bid organization meant explicitly targeting the people disadvantaged by apartheid, and this was to be accomplished by providing services to those communities that were left behind during apartheid and redesigning the city in order to break down the old barriers and provide new linkages among the communities. In different places in the bid document, human development included housing, jobs, and empowerment and variously referred to basic needs, education, and human rights (Hiller 2000, 442). The goal of the bid was to make Cape Town a more humane city, and the bid provided nine avenues for achieving this.

- The bid was going to be a catalyst, but in concert with other activities undertaken by the government such as upgrading the transportation network and the recreation facilities available to disadvantaged areas. Because of the Olympic timetable, this would also serve to accelerate these activities (445).

- Nearly 86% of the sports facilities were designated for disadvantaged areas, and would serve as "multipurpose community facilities" before and after the games (446).

- After the Olympic development started, the hope was that new housing, retail, and other community investments would occur (446).

- The new community sports facilities would enhance pride in the community, and serve to reduce the rate of crime (446).

- The projected 90,000 jobs across the country would be the single largest contribution to human development, and would work in concert with the central government's Affirmative Procurement Policy and other measures (447).

- Olympic housing needs would also provide housing units for nearly 30,000 people, which would be converted to local use after the games (447).

- The local bid company offered 50% of its business to commercial and professional services from formerly disadvantaged populations (448).

- The Olympics would accelerate transportation plans that were already drawn for implementation, and nearly 70% of these linked disadvantaged areas to the rest of the metropolitan area (449).

- Olympic community consultation reached new heights with the requirement that Strategic Environmental Assessments would be submitted to the community for ratification, although the implementation of this measure was limited (449).

The Cape Town bid also had political ramifications for the newly elected ANC. Although the bid originated under a local businessman, Pic-N-Pay owner Raymond Ackerman, who made the initial decisions and paid for them in 1993, the South African National Olympic Committee waited until after the elections in 1994 to support the bid only if the new national government supported it (Hiller 1997). This led to the ANC and a coalition of other political parties, business groups and other interests becoming the power behind the bid, particularly since the first post-apartheid local elections in Cape Town took place in 1996. Furthermore, in the 1996 local elections, the National Party won the majority of votes, which led to an uneasy relationship between the central and provincial government (Hiller 2000, 451).

Although the 2004 Olympics were held in Athens, Greece, Cape Town ranked third in the Olympic competition, surprising even the most ardent prognosticators. In retrospect, had Cape Town won the bid, additional strain on the capacity of the public service would have resulted. While the issues of administrative capabilities are still being worked out, the 2010 deadline for the World Cup will test the skills of the public service, and give the government an opportunity to create a new future for South Africa.

Culture and the Legacy of Apartheid

South African society is still smarting from the legacy of apartheid. How this legacy affects the transformation of the nation continues to be an evolving situation. In the introduction to this chapter, we noted that Daryl Glaser identified what he thought were four potential unifiers in post-apartheid South Africa: the English language as the accepted medium for communication; Christianity; Western-style consumerism; and international sporting competitions (Glaser 2003). The brief review of the structure of government, the role of change agents, the rise and demise of the RDP, the Ncholo Report on the condition of the public service, and the Cape Town 2004 bid for the Olympic games illustrate the deep-rooted nature of culture's impact on politics. Highlighting the questions that an interpretive perspective brings identifies the scope and scale that problem definitions and policy solutions ought to approach. Whether they can, or do, is the challenge. Can the English language function as a medium for communication in South Africa? It probably can. Can it serve as a unifier for the nation? That depends on the future one sees. Certainly, the impact of Christianity on the African continent can't be underestimated. The same holds true of Western-style consumerism. But both Christianity and consumerism, among the flows of globalization (Appadurai 1990), have been mediated as they are practiced on the continent in general, and in South Africa in particular. The Cape Town bid probably did more to highlight the amenities in Cape Town (relative to other cities vying for tourism development) than anything else, but the World Cup is coming and provides an opportunity to focus on identity issues rather than the narrow economic issues (with powerful allies in support) associated with the "Washington consensus."

The question of identity, and molding one, is what is most important about the possibility of unifying post-apartheid South Africa. Whether in the public service, the elected government, or in society as a whole, "society's forms are culture's substance" (Geertz 1973, 28). In an examination of the effect of racial differences on democratic legitimacy in South Africa at the beginning of the transition period, James Gibson found that support for democratic institutions varied, and Africans were less supportive than Whites. In the survey, Gibson asked questions that addressed four aspects of democracy: support for a multiparty system, political tolerance, relative valuation of order and liberty, and the importance of competitive elections. In general, he found that the political culture of the new nation is not democratic, and that outside of White South Africans, other racial groups did not embrace democratic institutions and processes. Furthermore, across all racial groups, those South Africans who feel that group solidarity is important are less supportive of democratic institutions. Unlike in the former Soviet Union and Eastern Europe, Gibson found that education did not play an important role in determining support for democratic values in South Africa. He speculated that this was due to the effects of apartheid in the education system (Gibson 2003, 797). These attitudes will play a crucial role in the trajectory of democratization and how developmental and decentralization policies are designed and implemented in the coming years. These should also be included as a part of the framework for discussing alternatives.

South Africa's cultural palimpsest, overwritten by success forces of colonization, apartheid, and now "democracy," illustrates the hidden dimension of culture. How government, society, and the global economy work in South Africa will continue to be mediated through the experiences of South Africans. Can government in general, and the public service, in particular, meet the needs of the South African people and serve as an agent of development? We have argued that bringing South African culture directly into the framework of discussion and debate will result in asking more appropriate questions about the future of this nation before designing solutions to resolve its challenges.

References

Adams, John. 2002. Culture and economic development in south Asia. *The Annals of the American Academy of Political and Social Science* 573, no. 1(January): 152-175.

African News Service. 2002. Scholars suggest upgrading culture to facilitate economic development. March 16, 2002: 1-4; http://www.comtexnews.com.

Africa Today. Editorial, 1993. Prospects for institutionalized democracy. *Africa Today* 40, no. 1: 7.

Agranoff, Robert, Jabu Sindane, and Ian Liebenberg. 2000. Sharing power? Intergovernmental relations in democratic transitions. In *Consolidation of democracy in Africa: A view from the south,* ed. Hussein Solomon and Ian Liebenberg, 267-300. Burlington, VT: Ashgate.

Ake, Claude. 1996. *Democracy and development in Africa.* Washington, D.C.: Brookings Institution.

Alexander, Neville. 2003. *An ordinary country: Issues in the transition from apartheid to democracy in South Africa.* New York: Berghahn Books.

Allaire, Yvan, and Mihaela Firsirotu. 1985. How to implement radical strategies in large organizations. *Sloan Management Review* 26 (Spring): 19-34.

Allen, Charlotte. 1998. Confucius and the scholars. *Atlantic Monthly* (April): 79-83.

Almond, Gabriel A. 1996. The civic culture: Prehistory, retrospect, and prospect. Irvine, CA: University of California, Irvine. *Center for the Study of Democracy, Research Paper Series in Empirical Democratic Theory, no. 1.*

Almond, Gabriel A., and Sydney Verba. 1963. *The civic culture.* Princeton: Princeton University Press.

American Institutes of Research. 1974. Assessing the impact of participant training on the attainment of developmental goals, Phase I: Methodological research. Washington, D.C.: American Institute for Research.

Appadurai, Arjun. 1990. Disjuncture and difference in the global cultural economy. *Theory, Culture, and Society* 7: 295-310.

Arango, Jorge. 1970. *The urbanization of the earth.* Boston: Beacon Press.

Argyris, Chris. 1991. *Organizational learning.* Reading, MA: Addison-Wesley.

Arnstein, Sherry. 1969. A ladder of citizen participation. *Journal of the American Institute of Planners* 35: 216-224.

Ashtor, E. 1976. *A social economic history of the Near East in the Middle Ages.* London: Collins.

Ayoade, John 1989. The culture debate in Africa. *The Black Scholar* 20 (Summer/Fall): 2-7.

Baker, Kendall L., Russell J. Dalton, and Kai Hildebrandt. 1981. *Germany transformed: Political culture and the new politics.* Cambridge, MA: Harvard University Press.

Baker, Randall. 1991. The role of the state and the bureaucracy in development since World War II. In *Handbook of comparative and development public administration,* ed. Ali Farazmand, 353-363. New York: Marcel Dekker.

Balogun, M. Jide. 1989. The role of management training institutions in developing the capacity for economic recovery and long-term growth in Africa. In *Economic structuring and African public administration,* ed. M. Jide Balogun and Gelase Mutahaba, 225-238. West Hartford, CT: Kumarian Press.

Bardhill, John, and James Cobbe. 1985. *Lesotho profiles.* Boulder, CO: Westview.

Barnard, Chester I. 1968. *The functions of the executive. 30th Anniv. Ed.* Cambridge, MA: Harvard University Press.

Bates, Ralph J. 1984. Toward a critical practice of educational administration. In *Leadership and organizational culture,* ed. Thomas J. Sergiovanni and John E. Corbally, 260-274. Urbana: University of Illinois Press.

Bayart, Jean-Francoise, Stephen Ellis, and Beatrice Hibou. 1999. *The criminalization of the state in Africa.* Trans. Stephen Ellis. Bloomington: Indiana University Press.

Berger, Peter. 1997. Four faces of global culture. *National Interest* 49: 23-29.

Berger, Peter, and Samuel P. Huntington, eds. 2002. *Many globalizations: Cultural diversity in the contemporary world.* New York: Oxford University Press.

Bishop, Clyde. 1977. Culture and the black administrator. In *Public administration and public policy: A minority perspective,* ed. Lawrence Howard, Lenneal Henderson, and Deryl Hunt, 113-120. Pittsburgh, PA: Public Policy Press.

Bjur, Wesley E., and Asghar, Zomorrodian. 1986. Towards indigenous theories of administration: An international perspective. *International Review of Administrative Sciences* 52: 397-420.

Black, Cyril E. 1966. *The dynamics of modernization.* New York: Harper and Row.

Blake, R. R., and Mouton, J. S. 1969. *Grid organization development.* Reading, MA: Addison-Wesley.

Bolman, Lee G., and Terrence E. Deal. 1991. Reframing organizations: *Artistry, choice, and leadership.* San Francisco, CA: Jossey-Bass.

Booth, Alan R. 1983. *Swaziland: Tradition and change in the southern African Kingdom.* Boulder, CO: Westview.

Bornstein, Lisa. 2000. Institutional context. In Poverty and inequality in South Africa: *Meeting the challenge,* ed. Julian May, 173-206. Cape Town: David Philip Publishers.

Brandt, Willy. 1980. *Report of the independent commission on international development issues, North-South: A program for survival.* Cambridge, MA: MIT Press.

Bratton, Michael. 1999. Second elections in Africa. In *Democratization in Africa,* ed. Larry Diamond and Marc F. Plattner, 18-33. Baltimore: Johns Hopkins University Press.

Brinkerhoff, Derick W., and Jennifer M. Coston. 1999. International development management in a globalized world. *Public Administration Review* 59: 346-361.

Briscoe, A., ed. 1995. *Local government finance, planning and business promotion.* Gaborone, Botswana: Friedrich Ebert Stitfung.

Bryant, Coralie, and Louise G. White. 1982. *Managing development in the Third World*. Boulder, CO: Westview Press.

Buchanan, Bruce, II. 1975. Red tape and the service ethic: Some unexpected differences between public and private managers. *Administration and Society* 6: 423-444.

Burbank, Matthew J., Gregory D. Andranovich, and Charles H. Heying. 2001. *Olympic dreams: The impact of mega-events on local politics*. Boulder, CO: Lynne Rienner.

Burger, David. 2002. *South Africa yearbook 2002/03*. Pretoria: Government Communications and Information System. http://www.info.gov.za/structure/parliament.htm (1 June 2004).

_____. 2002. *South Africa yearbook 2002/03*. Pretoria: Government Communications and Information System. http://www.info.gov.za/structure/pubserve.htm (1 June 2004).

Burrell, Gibson, and Gareth Morgan. 1979. *Sociological paradigms and organizational analysis*. London: Heinmann.

Butler, Anthony. 2004. *Contemporary South Africa*. New York: Macmillan/Palgrave.

Cabral, Amilcar. 1979. *Unity and struggle*. New York: Monthly Review Press.

Caiden, Gerald E., and Naomi J. Caiden. 1977. Administrative corruption. *Public Administration Review* 37: 301-309.

Caiden, Gerald, O. P. Dwivedi, and Joseph Jabbra, eds. 2001. *Where corruption lives*. Bloomfield, CT: Kumarian Press.

Caiden, Naomi J. 1991. Unanswered questions: Planning and budgeting in poor countries revisited. In *Handbook of comparative and development public administration*, ed. Ali Farazmand, 421-434. New York: Marcel Dekker.

Callaghy, Timothy M. 2000. Africa and the world political economy: More caught between a rock and a hard place. In *Africa in world politics: The African state system in flux*, 3d ed. John W. Harbeson, ed., and Donald Rothchild, 43-82. Boulder, CO: Westview.

Cason, Ronald W. 1981. *Language, culture, and cognition: Anthropological perspectives*. New York: Macmillan.

CIA-World Factbook. 2000. http://www.cia.gov/cia/publications/factbook/geos/sf.html

CIA-World Factbook, 2003. http://www.cia.gov/cia/publications/factbook/geos/sf.html

Chabal, Patrick. 1996. The African crisis: Context and interpretation. In *Postcolonial identities in Africa*, ed. Richard Werbner and Terence Ranger, 29-54. London: Zed Books.

Chabal, Patrick, and Jean-Pascal Daloz. 1999. *Africa works: Disorder as political instrument*. Bloomington: Indiana University Press.

Cheneaux-Repond, Kanengoni, Maia and Stan Kanengoni. 1995. *Some strengths and weaknesses of Botswana's development at local authority level*. Gaborone, Botswana: Friedrich Ebert Stitfung.

Chilcote, Ronald H. 1974. Dependency: *A critical synthesis of the literature*. Penguin: London.

Child, John D. 1981. Cultures, contingency and capitalism in the cross-national study of organizations. In *Research in organization behavior*, ed. Larry C.

Cummings, and Barry M. Staw, 303-356. Greenwich, CT: JAI Press.

Cleague, Christopher, Suzanne Gleason, and Stephen Knack. 2001. Determinants of lasting democracy in poor countries: Culture, development, and institutions. *The Annals of the American Academy of Political and Social Science*, January 2001: 14.

Cochrane, Glynn. 1983. Policies for strengthening local government in developing countries. Washington, D.C.: World Bank. *Staff Working Paper No. 582.*

Cohen, Paul S. 1969. Theories of myth. *Man* 17: 1-25.

Colclough, Christopher, and Stephen McCarthy. 1980. *The political economy of Botswana*. New York: Oxford University Press.

Comrade capitalist. 60 Minutes, April 26, 2004 http://www.cbsnews.com/stories/2004/04/26/60minutes/main613700.shtml (22 May 2004).

Conrad, Charles. 1983. Organizational power: Faces and symbolic forms. In *Communication and organizations: An interpretive approach*, ed. Linda L. Putnam and Michael E. Pacanowsky, 173-194. Thousand Oaks: Sage.

Conyers, Diana. 1983. Decentralization: The latest fashion in development administration. *Public Administration and Development* 3: 97-109.

Coulson, Andrew. 1982. *Tanzania: A political economy*. New York: Oxford University Press.

Crase, Lin, and Brian Dollery. 1999. Economic growth, administrative reform and the Ncholo report in the new South Africa. University of New England, Armidale NSW, Australia: *School of Economic Studies*, No. 99-2 http://www.une.edu.au/febl/Economics/Publications/ecowps.htm (3 May 2004).

Crozier, Michel. 1964. *The bureaucratic phenomenon*. Chicago: University of Chicago Press.

Cumming, Gordon. 2001. *Aid to Africa*. Burlington, VT: Ashgate.

Dahlgren, Stefan, Tyrrell Duncan, Allan Gustafsson, and Patrick Molutsi. 1993. *SIDA development assistance in Botswana: 1966-1993*. Gaborone, Botswana: SIDA.

Danevard, Andreas. 1995. Responsiveness in Botswana politics: Do elections matter? *Journal of Modern Africa Studies* 33: 3.

Daniel, Philip. 1979. *Africanization, nationalization and inequality*. New York: Cambridge University Press.

Darch, Colin. 1985. *Tanzania: World bibliographical series*. Santa Barbara, CA: University of California Press.

Davis, Stanley M. 1984. *Managing corporate culture*. Cambridge, MA: Ballinger.

Deal, Terrence E., and Allan A. Kennedy. 1982. *Corporate cultures: The rites and rituals of corporate life*. Reading, MA: Addison-Wesley.

De Guzman, Raul P., Mila A. Reforma, D.R. Reyos, and A. Kouzmin. 1991. Public management in the 1990s: An agenda of change. In *Public management in the 1990s*, ed. G. Bahadur, Narindar Pradhan, and Mila A. Reforma, 3-8. Manila: Eastern Regional Organization for Public Administration.

Deng, Francis M., and Terrence Lyons, eds. 1998. *African reckoning: A quest for good governance*. Washington, D.C.: Brookings Institution.

Denhardt, Robert B. 1993. *The pursuit of significance: Strategies for managerial success in public organizations*. Belmont, CA: Wadsworth.

Deutsch, Karl W. 1961. Social mobilization and political development. *American Political Science Review* 55: 493-514.

Diamond, Larry, and Marc F. Plattner, eds. 1999. *Democratization in Africa*. Baltimore: Johns Hopkins University Press.

Dierkes, Meinolf, Hans N. Weiler, and Arian B. Antal. 1987. *Comparative policy research: Learning from experience*. Brookfield, VT: Gower.

Doi, Takeo. 1973. *The anatomy of dependence*. Trans. John Bester. Tokyo: Kodansha International.

Dos Santos, T. 1970. The structure of dependence. *American Economic Review* 60: 231-236.

Dresang, Dennis L. 1984. *Public personnel management and public policy*. Boston: Little, Brown and Company.

Durham, Deborah. 1999. Civil lives: Leadership and accomplishment in Botswana. In *Civil society and the political imagination in Africa: Critical perspectives*, ed. John L. Comaroff, and Jean Comaroff, 192-218. Chicago: University of Chicago Press.

Dwivedi, O.P. 1999. Development administration: An overview. In *Bureaucracy and the alternatives in world perspective*, ed. Keith M. Henderson, and O.P. Dwivedi, 3-24. New York: St. Martin's Press.

Dwivedi, O.P., and J. Neff. 1982. Crises and continuities in development theory and administration. *Public Administration and Development* 2: 59-77.

Dwivedi, O.P., and Keith M. Henderson. 1990. State of the art: Comparative public administration and development administration. In *Public administration in world perspective*, ed. O.P. Dwivedi, and Keith M. Henderson, 9-20. Ames, IA: Iowa State University Press.

Eckstein, Harry. 1966. *Division and cohesion in democracy*. Princeton: Princeton University Press.

————. 1988. A culturalist theory of political change. *American Political Science Review* 82: 789-804.

————. 1990. Political culture and political change. *American Political Science Review* 84: 253-258.

————. 1996. Lessons for the 'third wave' from the first. Irvine, CA: University of California, Irvine. *Center for the Study of Democracy, Research Paper Series in Empirical Democratic Theory, No. 2*.

Eisenstadt, Shmuel Noah. 1964. Continuity of modernization and development of administration: Preliminary statement of the problem (*CAG Occasional Papers*). Bloomington, IA: Indiana University Press.

Elashmawi, Farid, and Philip R. Harris. 1993. *Multicultural management: New skills for global success*. Houston, TX: Gulf Publishing Company.

Elliott, Jaques 1990. In Praise of Hierarchy, *Harvard Business Review* (January-February 1990). In *Classics of Organizational Theory 5th Edition*, pp. 234-241, by Jay M. Shafritz and J. Steven Ott, editors. New York: Harcourt. College Publishers.

Esman, Milton J. 1988. The maturing of development administration. *Public Administration and Development* 8: 125-134.

————. 1966. The CAG and the study of administration: A mid-term appraisal (*CAG Occasional Papers*). Bloomington: Indiana University Press.

_____. 1974. Administrative doctrine and developmental needs. In *Administration of change in Africa*, ed. E.P. Morgan, 3-26. New York: Dunellen.

_____. 1991. *Management dimensions in development*. West Hartford, CT: Kumarian Press.

Etounga-Manguelle, Daniel. 2000. Does Africa need a culture adjustment program? In *Culture matters: How values shape human progress*, ed. Lawrence E. Harrison and Samuel P. Huntington, 65-77. New York: Basic Books.

Etzioni, Amatai. 1975. *A comparative analysis of complex organizations, rev. ed.* New York: The Free Press.

Everd, Robert. 1983. The language of organizations: The case of the navy. In *Organizational symbolism*, ed. R. Pondy, P.J. Frost, G. Morgan and T.C. Dandridge, 125-143. Greenwich, CT: JAI Press.

Fayol, Henri. 1949. *General and industrial management*. Trans. Constance Storrs. London: Pitman Publishing Ltd.

Filatova, Irina. 2000. Democracy versus state: The African dilemma? In *Consolidation of democracy in Africa: A view from the south*, ed. Hussein Solomon and Ian Liebenberg, 11-44. Burlington, VT: Ashgate.

Fisiy, C., and P. Geschiere. 1996. Witchcraft, violence and identity: Different trajectories in postcolonial Cameroon. In *Postcolonial identities in Africa*, ed. Richard Werbner and Terrence Ranger, 193-221. London: Zed Books.

Fivars, Grace. 1980. *The critical incident technique: A bibliography*, 2d ed. Palo Alto: American Institutes of Research.

Flanagan, John C. 1949. Critical requirements: A new approach to employee evaluation. *Personnel Psychology* 2: 419-425.

Ford, David. Jr. 1978. Cultural influences on organizational behavior. *Social Change* 8:1.

Frank, Andre Gunder. 1966. The development of underdevelopment. *Monthly Review* 18 (Sept.): 17-31.

Friedmann, John. 1992. *Empowerment: The politics of alternative development*. Cambridge, MA: Basil Blackwell.

Galbraith, John Kenneth. 1958. *The Affluent Society*. Boston: Houghton-Mifflin.

Galtung, Johan. 1971. A structural theory of imperialism. *Journal of Peace Research* 2: 81-116.

Gaus, John M. 1936. *American society and public administration. The frontiers of public administration.* Chicago: University of Chicago Press.

_____. 1940. A theory of organization in public administration. In *The frontiers of public administration*, 66-91. Chicago: The University of Chicago Press.

Geertz, Clifford. 1973. *The interpretation of cultures*. New York: Basic Books.

Gertzel, Cherry, ed. 1984. *The dynamics of one-party state in Zambia*. Manchester, UK: Manchester University Press.

Gibson, James L. 2003. The legacy of apartheid: Racial differences in the legitimacy of democratic institutions and processes in the new South Africa. *Comparative Political Studies* 36: 772-800.

Giddens, Anthony. 1990. *The consequences of modernity*. Palo Alto: Stanford University Press.

Giordano, Joseph, and Giordano, Grace. 1976. Ethnicity and community mental health. *Community Mental Health* 1.

Glaser, Daryl. 2001. *Politics and society in South Africa*. Thousand Oaks: Sage.

Goffman, Erving. 1959. *The presentation of self in everyday life.* New York: Doubleday.
_____. 1967. Interaction ritual. Garden City, NY: Anchor Books.
Gortner, Harold F., Julianne Mahler, and Jean Bell Nicholson. 1987. *Organization theory: A public perspective.* Chicago: Dorsey Press.
Gottdiener, Mark, and Alexandros Lagopoulos, ed. 1986. *The city and the sign: An introduction to urban semiotics.* New York: Columbia University Press.
Grindle, Merilee, ed. 1980. *Politics and policy implementation in the Third World.* New Jersey: Princeton University Press.
Gulick, Luther, and Lyndall Urwick, eds. 1937. *Papers on the science of administration.* New York: Columbia University Institute of Public Administration.
Hall, Edward T. 1959. *The silent language.* Garden City, NY: Doubleday.
_____. 1963. *Hidden dimensions.* Garden City, NY: Doubleday.
_____. 1987. *Hidden differences.* Garden City, NY: Anchor Press.
Hall, Richard H. 1977. *Organizations: Structure and process, 2d ed.* Englewood Cliffs, NJ: Prentice-Hall.
Hancock, Donald M. 1983. Comparative public policy: An assessment. In *Political science: The state of the discipline,* ed. Ada W. Finifter, 283-302. Washington, D.C.: American Political Science Association.
Haque, Shamsul M. 1996. The contextless nature of public administration in Third World countries. *International Review of Administrative Sciences* 62: 315-329.
Haragopal, G., and Prasad, V.S. 1990. Social bases of administrative culture in India. *Indian Journal of Public Administration* 36: 384-397.
Harbeson, John W. 2000. Externally assisted democratization: Theoretical issues and African realities. In *Africa in world politics: The African state system in flux, 3d ed.* Ed. John W. Harbeson, and Donald Rothchild, 235-259. Boulder, CO: Westview.
Harrison, Lawrence E. 1992. *Who prospers? How cultural values shape economic and political success.* New York: Basic Books.
Hartland-Thurnberg, Penelope. 1978. *Botswana: An African growth economy.* Boulder, CO: Westview.
Haugerud, Angelique. 1995. *The culture of politics in modern Kenya.* New York: Cambridge University Press.
Hayakawa, S.I. 1953. *Symbol, status and personality.* New York: Harcourt Brace.
Heady, Ferrel. 1989. Issues in comparative and international administration. In *Handbook of public administration,* ed. Jack Rabin, W. Bartley Hildreth, and Gerald J. Miller, 499-521. New York: Marcel Dekker.
_____. 1991. *Public administration: A comparative perspective, 4th ed.* New York: Marcel Dekker.
_____. 1998. Comparative and international public administration: Building intellectual bridges. *Public Administration Review* 58: 32-39.
Henderson, Errol A. 1998. The impact on culture on African coups d'etat, 1960-1997. *World Affairs* 161: 10-21.
Hertzberg, Frederick, Bernard Mausner, and Barbara Bloch Snyderman. 1959. *The motivation to work, 2d ed.* New York: John Wiley.
Hicks, Norman, and Paul Streeten. 1979. Indicators of development: The search for a basic needs yardstick. *World Development* 7: 567-589.

Hiller, Harry H. 1997. And if Cape Town loses? Mega-events and the Olympic candidature. *Indicator South Africa* 14 (3).

————. 2000. Mega-events, urban boosterism and growth strategies: An analysis of the objectives and legitimations of the Cape Town 2004 Olympic bid. *International Journal of Urban and Regional Research* 24: 439-458.

Hofstede, Geert. 1980. Motivation, leadership, and organization: Do American theories apply abroad? *Organization Dynamics 9* (summer): 42-63.

————. 1993. Cultural dimensions in people management: The socialization perspective. In *Globalizing management: Creating and leading the competitive organization,* ed. Vlademir Pucik, Noel M. Tichy, and Carole K. Barnett, 139-158. New York: John Wiley.

Holm, John D. 1987. Botswana: A paternalistic democracy. *World Affairs* 150: 21-30.

Hood, Christopher. 1998. *The art of the state: Culture, rhetoric and public management.* Oxford: Clarendon Press.

Howard, Lawrence. C., Lenneal J. Henderson, and Daryl Hunt. 1977. *Public administration and public policy: A minority perspective.* Pittsburgh, PA: Public Policy Press.

Hummel, Ralph. 1986. *The bureaucratic experience,* 4th ed. New York: St. Martin's Press.

Huntington, Samuel P. 1968. *Political order in changing societies.* New Haven: Yale University Press.

————. 1965. Political development and political decay. *World Politics* 17: 386-430.

————. 1993. The clash of civilizations. *Foreign Affairs* 72, no. 3: 22-49.

Hyden, Goran. 1983. *No shortcuts to progress.* Berkeley, CA: University of California Press.

————. 1989. Community governance and high politics. In *Beyond autocracy in Africa: Working paper for the inaugural seminar of the governance in African programme,* ed. Richard Joseph, 2-6. Atlanta: Carter Center.

————. 1999. Governance and the reconstitution of political order. In *State, conflict, and democracy in Africa,* ed. Richard Joseph, 179-195. Boulder, CO: Lynne Rienner.

Hyden, Goran, Dele Olowu, and Hastings W. O. Okoth-Ogendo. 2000. *African perspecties on governance.* Trenton, NJ: Africa World Press.

Hyden, Goran, and Rwekaza Mukandala. 1999. *Agencies in foreign aid: Comparing China, Sweden and the United States in Tanzania.* New York: St. Martin's Press.

Ingersoll, Virginia H., and Guy B. Adams. 1992. *The tacit organization.* Greenwich, CT: JAI Press.

Inglehart, Ronald, and Wayne E. Baker. 2000. Modernization, cultural change, and the persistence of traditional values. *American Sociological Review* 65: 19-51.

Ingold, Tim, ed. 1994. *Companion encyclopedia of anthropology.* New York: Routledge.

Inkeles, Alex, and David H. Smith. 1974. Becoming modern. In *Becoming modern: Individual change in six developing countries.* Cambridge, MA: Harvard University Press.

Inzerilli, Giorgio, and Andre Laurent. 1983. Managerial views of organization structure in France and the U.S.A. *International Studies of Management and Organization* 13, no.1-2: 97-118.

Jones, Merrick L. 1989. Management development: An African focus. *International Studies of Management and Organization* 19 (1): 74-90.

Joseph, Sarah. 1998. Interrogating culture: *Critical perspectives on contemporary social theory.* New Delhi: Sage.

Jreisat, Jamil E. 1991. Bureaucratization of the Arab world: Incompatible influences. In *Handbook of comparative and development public administration,* ed. Ali Farazmand, 665-75. New York: Marcel Dekker.

Jun, Jong S. 1993. What is philosophy? Administration? *Administrative Theory and Praxis* 15, no.1: 46-52.

_____. 2003. Transcending the limits of comparative administration and a new internationalism in the making. Unpublished paper.

Jun, Jong S., and Muto, Hiromi. 1995. The hidden dimensions of Japanese administration: Culture and its impact. *Public Administration Review* 55: 125-134.

_____. 1976. Renewing the study of comparative administration: Some reflections on current possibilities. *Public Administration Review* 36: 141-47.

Kasfir, Nelson. 1999. "No-party democracy" in Uganda. In *Democratization in Africa,* ed. Larry Diamond, and Marc F. Plattner, 201-215. Baltimore: Johns Hopkins University Press.

Kautsky, John H. 1972. *The political consequences of modernization.* New York: Wiley.

Khanna, Kuldip. 1974. Contemporary models of public administration: An assessment of their utility and exposition of their inherent fallacies. *Philippine Journal of Public Administration* 18, no. 2: 103-125.

Kiggundu, Moses N. 1989. *Managing organizations in developing countries.* West Hartford, CT: Kumarian Press.

Kim, Kihwan. 1980. *Papers on the political economy of Tanzania.* London: Praeger Publishers.

Koehn, Peter. 1989. Local government involvement in national development planning: Guidelines for project selection based upon Nigeria's fourth plan experience. *Public Administration and Development* 9: 417-436.

Koelble, Thomas A. 1999. The global economy and democracy in South Africa. New Brunswick, NJ: Rutgers University Press.

Korten, David C. 1980. Community organizations and rural development: A learning process approach. *Public Administration Review* 40: 480-511.

Kreps, G. 1984. Organizational culture and organizational development: Promoting flexibility in an urban hospital. Paper presented at the meeting of the International Communication Association Convention, San Francisco, CA.

Kumbula, Tendayi J. 1979. *Education and social control in southern Rhodesia.* Palo Alto: R & E Research Associates.

Kurian, George T. 1987. *Encyclopedia of the Third World,* 3d ed. New York: Facts on File.

Kurtz, Laura S. 1978. *Historical dictionary of Tanzania.* Metuchen, NJ: Scarecrow Press.

Lal, Deepak. 1998. *Unintended consequences: The impact of factor endowments, culture, and politics on long run economic performance.* Cambridge, MA: MIT Press.

Landau, Martin. 1969. Redundancy, rationality and the problem of duplication and overlap. *Public Administration Review* 29: 346-58.

Landes, David S. 1998. *The wealth and poverty of nations: Why some are so rich and some so poor.* New York: W.W. Norton.

Lasswell, Harold. 1936. Politics: *Who gets what, when, how?* New York: McGraw-Hill.

Lau, A.W., Newman, A.R. and Broedling, L.A. 1980. The Nature of Managerial Work in the Public Sector. *Public Administration Review,* 40, 5: 513-520.

LeMarchand, Rene, and Keith Legg. 1972. Political clientelism and development: A preliminary analysis. *Comparative Politics* 4: 149-178.

Leonard, David K. 1991. *African successes: Four public managers of Kenyan rural development.* Berkeley: University of California Press.

Lester, David. 1997. Suicide in American Indians. Commack, NY: *Nova Science.*

Lindblom, Charles E., and David K. Cohen. 1979. *Usable knowledge: Social science and social problem solving.* New Haven, CT: Yale University Press.

Lippit, Gordon L., Peter Langseth, and Jack Mossop. 1985. *Implementing organizational change.* San Francisco: Jossey-Bass.

Lodge, Tom. 2003. *Politics in South Africa.* Bloomington: Indiana University Press.

Louis, Meryl R. 1980. Surprise and sense-making: What newcomers experience in entering unfamiliar organizational settings. *Administrative Science Quarterly* 25: 226-251.

————. 1980. Organizations as culture bearing milieu. In *Organizational symbolism,* ed. Louis R. Pondy, Peter J. Frost, Gareth Morgan, and Thomas C. Dandridge, 39-54. Greenwich, CT: JAI Press.

Luke, David F. 1986. Trends in development administration: The state in the Third World. *Public Administration and Development* 6: 73-85.

Mahler, Julianne. 1977. Influences of organizational culture on learning in public agencies. *Journal of Public Administration Research and Theory* 7: 519-540.

Maslow, Abraham. 1943. A theory of human motivation. *Psychological Review* 50: 370-396.

May, Julian, ed. 2000. *Poverty and inequality in South Africa: Meeting the challenge.* Cape Town: David Philip Publishers.

McClelland, David C. 1961. *The achieving society.* Princeton, NJ: Van Nostrand.

————. 1963. The achievement motive in economic growth. In *Industrialization and society,* ed. Bert Hoselitz and Wilbert E. Moore, 74-79. Paris: UNESCO.

McCurdy, Howard E. 1977. *Public administration: A synthesis.* Menlo Park, CA: Cummings Publishing Company, Inc.

McDonogh, Peter, Samuel Barnes, and Antonio L. Pina. 1995. The nature of political support and legitimacy in Spain. *Comparative Political Science* 27: 349-380.

Meissner, Martin. 1976. The language of work. In *Handbook of work, organization and society,* ed. R. Rubin, 205-279. Chicago: Rand McNally.

Michie, Aruna. M. 1989. Decentralization and public welfare in India. Paper presented at the annual meeting of the Western Social Science Association, Albuquerque, April, 26-29.

Miles, Matthew B., and Michael Huberman. 1994. *Qualitative Data Analysis.* Thousand Oaks, CA: Sage.

Miles, Matthew B., and Richard A. Schmuck. 1971. Improving schools through organization development: An overview. In *Organizational development in schools,* ed. Richard A. Schmuck, and Matthew B. Miles, 7-12. Palo Alto, CA: National Press Books.

Mintzberg, Henry. 1979. *The structuring of organizations: A synthesis of the research.* Englewood Cliffs, NJ: Prentice-Hall.

_____. 1990. Strategy formation: Schools of thought. In *Perspectives on strategic management,* ed. James W. Frederickson, 105-236. New York: Harper Business.

Mokate, Renosi. 2000. Macro-economic context. In *Poverty and inequality in South Africa: Meeting the challenge,* ed. Julian May, 51-72. Cape Town: David Philip Publishers.

Montgomery, John D. 1974. *Technology and civil life.* Cambridge, MA: MIT Press.

_____. 1980. Administering to the poor (or if we cannot help the rich dictators, what can we do for the poor?). *Public Administration Review* 40: 421-25.

_____. 1985. The African manager. *Pakistani Management Review* (Second Quarter): 82-112.

_____. 1986A. Bureaucratic politics in southern Africa. *Public Administration Review* 46: 407-413.

_____. 1986B. Levels of managerial leadership in Southern Africa. *The Journal of Developing Areas* 21: 15-30.

_____. 1986C. Life at the apex: The functions of permanent secretaries in nine southern African countries. *Public Administration and Development* 6: 211-221.

_____. 1987A. Probing managerial behavior: Image and reality in southern Africa. *World Development* 15: 911-929.

_____. 1987B. How African managers serve developmental goals. *Comparative Politics* 19: 347-360.

_____. 1991. The strategic environment of public managers in developing countries. In *Handbook of comparative and development public administration,* ed. Ali Farazmand, 511-526. New York: Marcel Dekker.

Montgomery, John D., and Milton J. Esman. 1971. Popular participation in development administration. *Journal of Comparative Administration* 3: 359-383.

Morgan, Gareth. 1986. *Images of organizations.* Thousand Oaks: Sage.

Morgan, Philip. 1979. Managing development assistance: Some effects with special reference to southern Africa. Paper presented at the annual meeting of the African Studies Association, Los Angeles, CA, 1979.

_____. 1984. Development management and management development in Africa. *Rural Africana* 18 (winter): 3-15.

Moris, Jon R. 1977. The transferability of Western management concepts and programs: An east African perspective. In *Education and training for public sector management in developing countries,* ed. Lawrence D. Stifel, James S. Coleman, Joseph E. Black. 73-84. New York: Rockefeller Foundation.

Morley, Ilene E. 1984. On imagery and cycling of decision making. In *Leaders and managers: International perspectives on managerial behavior and leadership*, ed. James G. Hunt, Dian-Marie Hosking, Chester A. Schrieshheim, and Rosemary Stewart, 269-274. New York: Pergamon Press.

Mosher, Frederick. C. 1982. Public administration. In *Current issues in public administration, 2d ed.* Ed. Frederick S. Lane, 4-13. New York: St. Martin's Press.

Msabaha, Ibrahim S. R., and Timothy M. Shaw, eds. 1987. *Confrontation and liberation in southern Africa: Regional directions after the Nkomati accord.* Boulder, CO: Westview.

Mtewa, Mekki. 1984. *Malawi: Democratic theory and public policy.* Cambridge, MA: Oxford University Press.

Museveni, Yoweri K. 2000. *What is Africa's problem?* Elizabeth Kanyogonya, ed. Minneapolis: University of Minnesota Press.

Mushkin, Selma J., Frank H. Sandifer, and Sally Familton. 1978. *Current status of public management research conducted by or supported by federal agencies.* Washington, D.C.: Georgetown University, Public Services Laboratory.

Nakane, Chie. 1970. *The Japanese society.* Rutland, VT: Charles E. Tuttle.

National Association of Schools of Public Affairs and Administration (NASPAA). 1985. *Improving management in southern Africa: Final report to the regional training council of the southern African development coordinating conference.* Washington, D.C.: NASPAA.

Nonaka, Ikujiro, and Hirotaka Takeuchi. 1995. *The knowledge-creating company.* New York: Oxford University Press.

Norgaard, Richard B. 1994. *Development betrayed: The end of progress and a coevolutionary revisioning of the future.* London: Routledge.

Nti, J. 1989. The impact of economic crisis on the effectiveness of public service personnel. In *Economic restructuring and African public administration,* ed. Jide Balogun M., and Gelase Mutahaba, 121-129. West Hartford, CT: Kumarian Press.

Nyangoro, Julius Edo. 1989. *The state and the capitalist development in Africa: Declining political economies.* Westport, CT: Praeger.

Nyeko, Balan. 1982. *Swaziland: World bibliographical series.* Santa Barbara, CA: University of California Press.

Odhiambo, Atieno E.S. 2002. The cultural dimensions of development in Africa. *Africa Studies Review* 45, no. 3: 1-16.

Ojo, Olatunde. 1985. Regional cooperation and integration. In *African international relations,* ed. Olatunde Ojo, D.K. Orwa, and C.M.B. Utete, 142-183. New York: Longman.

Olowu, Dele. 1989. Local institutions and socio-economic development. *Canadian Journal of African Studies* 23: 201-231.

Olowu, Dele and Paul Smoke. 1992. Determinants of Success in African Local Governments: An Overview. *Public Administration and Development* 12 (1992): 1-7.

Osabu-Kle, Daniel T. 2000. *Compatible cultural democracy: The key to development in Africa.* Petersborough, Ontario: Broadview Press.

Osborne, David, and Ted Gaebler. 1992. *Reinventing government: How the entrepreneurial spirit is transforming the public sector.* Reading, MA: Addison-Wesley.

Ott, Steven J. 1989. *The organization culture perspective.* Pacific Grove, CA: Brooks Cole.

Palmer, Monte. 1985. *Dilemmas of political development, 3d ed.* Itasca, Illinois: F.E. Peacock Publishers.

Peters, B. Guy. 1990. The necessity and difficulty of comparison in public administration. *Asian Journal of Public Administration* 12, no. 1: 3-28.

————. 1989. *The politics of bureaucracy, 3d ed.* New York: Longman.

Peters, Thomas J., and Robert H. Waterman, Jr. 1982. *In search of excellence.* New York: Harper and Row.

Peters-Berries, Christian. 1995. *Aspects of local government finance in Botswana.* Goborone, Botswana: Friedrich Ebert Stitfung.

Pettigrew, Andre M. 1979. On studying organizational cultures. *Administrative Science Quarterly* 24: 570-581.

Pfiffner, John M., and Frank P. Sherwood. 1960. *Administrative organization.* Englewood Cliffs, NJ: Prentice Hall.

Picard, Louis A. 1987. *The politics of development in Botswana.* Gaborone, Botswana: Friedrich Ebert Stitfung.

Picard, Louis A., Athumani J. Liviga, and Michele Garrity. 1994. Sustainable policies, management capacity, and institutional development. In *Policy reform for sustainable development in Africa: The institutional imperative,* ed. Louis A. Picard, and Michele Garrity, 113-126. Boulder, CO: Lynne Reiner.

Pick, William. 1999. Health and security in sub-Saharan Africa. In *Common security and civil society in Africa,* ed. Lennart Wohlgemuth, Samantha Gibson, Stephan Klasen, and Emma Rothschild, 64-77. Stockholm: Nordiska Afrikainstitutet.

Pickering, Kathleen, and David Mushinski. 2001. Making the case for culture in economic development: A cross-sectional analysis of western tribes. *American Indian Culture and Research Journal* 25 (Winter): 45-65.

Polanyi, Michael. 1966. *The tacit dimension.* New York: Anchor Books.

Pondy, Louis. R., and Ian Mitroff. 1979. Beyond open systems models of organizations. In *Research in organizational behavior,* ed. Larry C. Cummings, and Barry M. Straw, 3-39. Greenwich, CT: JAI Press.

Posz, Gary, Bruce Janigan, and Jong S. Jun. 1994. Redesigning U.S. foreign aid. *SAIS Review* 14, no. 2: 159-169.

Potholm, Christian P. 1972. Swaziland: *The dynamics of political modernization.* Berkeley, CA: University of California Press.

Przeworski, Adam, and Henry Teune. 1982. *The Logic of Comparative Social Inquiry.* Malabar, FL: Robert E. Krieger Publishing Company.

Public Service Commission. 2000. *Survey of compliance with the Batho Pele policy.* Pretoria: Public Service Commission. http://psc.gov.za/docs/reports/2000/survey/ general.pdf (1 June 2004).

Pursley, Robert D., and Norman Snortland. 1980. *Managing government organizations.* North Scituate, MA: Duxbury Press.

Putnam, Linda L. 1983. Paradigms for organizational communication research: An overview and synthesis. *Western Journal of Speech Communication* 46: 192-206.

_____. 1983. The interpretive perspective: An alternative to functionalism. In *Communication and organizations: An interpretive approach*, ed. Linda L. Putnam, and Michael E. Pacanowsky, 31-54. Thousand Oaks: Sage.

Ramutsindela, Maano. 2001. *Unfrozen ground: South Africa's contested spaces.* Burlington, VT: Ashgate.

Reilly, William. 1987. Management and training for development: The hombe thesis. *Public Administration and Development* 7: 25-42.

Rice, Kenneth A. 1990. *Geertz and culture.* Ann Arbor: University of Michigan Press.

Rieger, Fritz. 1987. *The influence of national culture on organizational structure, process and strategic decision making: A study of international airlines.* Ph.D. diss., McGill University.

Riggs, Fred W. 1964. *Administration in developing countries: The theory of prismatic society.* Boston: Houghton Mifflin.

_____. 1976. The American tradition in public administration. Paper presented at the national conference of the American Society for Public Administration, Washington, D.C., April 1976.

_____. 1967. *The ecology of administration.* New York: Asia Publishing House.

_____. 1957. Agraria and industria: Toward a typology of public adminstration. In *Toward a comparative study of public administration*, ed. William J. Siffin. Bloomington, IN: Indiana University Press.

Roche, Maurice. 2000. *Mega-events and modernity: Olympics and expos in the growth of global culture.* New York: Routledge.

Ronan, N. 1993. Developing the African manager: The good, the bad and the competent. *Management Education and Development* 24: 388-394.

Rondinelli, Dennis A. 1983. *Development projects as policy experiments.* New York: Methuen.

Rondinelli, Dennis, John Nellis, and Shabbir Cheema. 1984. Decentralization in developing countries. Washington, D.C.: World Bank, *Staff Working Paper*, No. 581.

Rostow, Walt W. 1965. *The economics of take-off into sustained growth. Proceedings of a conference held by the International Economic Association.* New York: St. Martin's Press.

Sandbrook, Richard. 2000. *Closing the circle: Democratization and development in Africa.* New York: Zed Books.

Sanders, Charles. L. 1980. Through a glass darkly: Implications of black culture for public administration. *The Bureaucrat* (Fall): 30-37.

Sassen, Saskia. 1996. Losing control? Sovereignty in an age of globalization. New York: Columbia University Press.

Sathe, Vijay. 1985. *Culture and related corporate realities: Text, cases, and readings on organizational entry, establishment, and change.* Homewood, IL: R.D. Irwin.

Schatzberg, Michael G. 1984. *The political economy of Zimbabwe.* New York: Praeger.

Schein, Edgar H. 1985. *Organizational culture and leadership.* San Francisco: Jossey-Bass.

Schon, Donald A. 1983. *The reflective practitioner: How professionals think in action.* New York: Basic Books.

Schwartz, Howard, and Davis, Stanley. 1981. Matching corporate culture and business strategy. *Organizational Dynamics* 10, (Summer 1981): 30-48.

Seddon, John W. 1985. The development of indigenization of Third World business: African values in the workplace. In *Current Research in Management,* ed. Valerie Hammond, 98-109. London: Frances Pinter Publishers.

Seekings, Jeremy. 2000. Introduction: Urban studies in South Africa after apartheid. *International Journal of Urban and Regional Research* 24: 832-840.

Seidman, Robert. 1979. Development planning and the legal order in black anglophonic Africa. *Studies in Comparative International Development* 14 (Summer): 13-27.

Selznick, Philip. 1957. *Leadership in administration: A sociological interpretation.* Evanston, IL: Row, Peterson.

Seppala, Pekka, and Bertha Koda. 1998. *The making of a periphery: Economic development and cultural encounters in southern Tanzania.* Uppsala: Nordiska Afrikainstitutet.

Sergiovanni, Thomas J., and John E. Corbally. 1984. Theory of practice in education administration and organizational analysis. In *Leadership and organizational culture,* ed. Thomas J. Sergiovanni, and John E. Corbally, 207-213. Urbana: University of Illinois Press.

Shafritz, Jay M., and Steven Ott J. 2001. *Classics of Organization Theory, 5th edition.* Olando, FL: Harcourt Brace.

Shapiro, Harry L. 1970. *Aspects of culture.* Freeport, NY: Books for Libraries Press.

Siehl, Caren, and Joanne Martin. 1984. The role of symbolic management: How can managers effectively transmit organizational culture? In *Leaders and managers: International perspectives on managerial behavior and leadership,* ed. James G. Hunt, Dian Marie Hosking, Chester A. Schriesheim, and Rosemary Stewart, 227-269. New York: Pergamon Press.

Siffin, William J. 2001. The problem of development. In *Handbook of comparative and development public administration,* ed. Ali Farazmand, 1-8. New York: Marcel-Dekker.

Silverman, David. 1970. *The theory of organizations.* London: Hinemann.

Simmons, A. M. 2001. Cheap drugs are only part of weapons against AIDS. *Los Angeles Times,* April 8, A-1,10-11.

Singer, Molly. 2000. Culture works: Cultural resources as economic development tools. *Public Management* August: 11-16.

Singh, J.P. 1986. Management events from India: A comparative study with African countries, Unpublished Seminar Paper, Cambridge, MA, Harvard University.

Smircich, Linda. 1983. Organizations as shared meanings. In *Organizational symbolism,* ed. Louis R. Pondy, Peter J. Frost, Gareth Morgan, and Thomas C. Dandridge, 55-65. Greenwich, CT: JAI Press.

Solomon, Hussein, and Ian Leibenberg, ed. 2000. *Consolidation of democracy in Africa: A view from the south.* Aldershot, U.K., Ashgate.

Sorenson, Georg. 1991. *Democracy, dictatorship and development.* Houndmills, UK: Macmillan. South Africa.
http://encarta.msn.com/encyclopedia_761557321/south_africa.html

Sowell, Thomas. 1994. *Race and culture: World view.* New York: Basic Books.

Steidlmeier, Paul. 1987. *The paradox of poverty: A reappraisal of economic development policy.* Cambridge, MA: Ballinger Publishing Co.

Stringer, Robert. A., Jr. 1966. Achievement motivation and management control. *Personnel Administration* 29 (Nov./Dec.): 3-5.

Subramanian, V., ed. 1990. *Public administration in the Third World: An international handbook.* New York: Greenwood Press.

Swedish International Development Agency. 1993. *Decentralization in Botswana: Policy paper and action plan.* Gaborone, Botswana: SIDA.

Swerdlow, Irving. 1975. *The public administration of economic development.* New York: Praeger.

Tagiuri, Renato, and George H. Litwin, eds. 1968. *Organizational climate: Exploration of a concept.* Boston: Harvard University, Graduate School of Business Administration, Division of Research.

Taylor, Edward B. 1924. *Primitive culture: Researches into the development of mythology, philosophy, religion, art and custom, 7th ed.* New York: Brentano's.

Taylor, Ian. 2002. Neo-liberalism and democracy: The role of intellectuals in South Africa's "democratic transition." In *Political cultures in democratic South Africa,* comp. Henning Melber, 34-49. Uppsala: Nordiska Afrikainstitutet.

Thompson, Carol B. 1986. *Challenge to imperialism: The frontline states in the liberation of Zimbabwe.* Boulder, CO: Westview.

Thompson, Leonard M. 1975. *Survival in two worlds: Moshoshoe of Lesotho.* New York: Clarendon Press.

Tichy, Noel M., and David O. Ulrich. 1984. The leadership challenge: A call for the transformational leader. *Sloan Management Review* 26 (Fall): 59-68.

Todaro, Michael P. 1977. *Economic development in the Third World: An introduction to problems and policies in global perspective.* London: Longman.

Tordoff, William, ed. 1975. *Politics in Zambia.* Berkeley, CA: University of California Press.

Tordoff, William. 1988. Local administration in Botswana. *Public Administration and Development* 8: 183-202.

Toure, Sekou. 1969. A dialectical approach to culture. *The Black Scholar* 1, (November): 23.

Trice, Harrison, and Janet Bayer. 1993. *The culture of work organizations.* Englewood Cliffs, NJ: Prentice-Hall.

Trujillo, Nick. 1983. Performing Mintzberg's roles: The nature of managerial communication. In *Communication and organizations: An interpretive approach,* ed. Linda L. Putnam, and Michael E. Pacanowsky, 73-98. Beverly Hills: Sage.

Turok, Ivan. 1995. Restructuring or reconciliation? South Africa's Reconstruction and Development Program. *International Journal of Urban and Regional Research* 19: 305-318.

Umeh, Ogwo J. 1990. *Differences in administrative characteristics among seven developing African countries.* Ph.D. diss. Texas Tech University.

_____. 1991. Determinants of administrative development in seven southern African countries. *The Indian Journal of Public Administration* 37 (Jan./Mar.): 47-61.

Umeh, Ogwo J., and Greg Andranovich. 1992. Capacity building and development administration in southern African countries. *International Review of Administrative Sciences* 58: 57-70.

_____. 2001. The conduct of managerialism and its performance in southern African countries. In *Handbook of Comparative and Development Public Administration*, 2d ed. Ed. Ali Farazmand, 521-533. New York: Marcel Dekker.

United Nations Educational Scientific and Cultural Organization (UNESCO). 2001. *Newsletter*. Switzerland: Swiss National Commission for UNESCO.

Uphoff, Norman, John Cohen, and Arthur Goldsmith. 1979. Feasibility and Application of Rural Development Participation: A State-of-the-Art Paper. Ithaca, N.Y.: Cornell University.

Uzodike, U. O. 1997. Democracy and economic reforms: Developing underdeveloped political economies. In *Democracy and democratization in Africa: Toward the 21st century*, ed. E. Ike Udogu, 21-38. New York: E.J. Brill.

Valdes, Julio Carranza. 2002. Culture and development: Some considerations for debate. Translated by Richard Stoller. *Latin American Perspectives* 29 (July): 31-46.

Valenzuela, Samuel J., and Arturo Valenzuela. 1978. Modernization and dependency: Alternative perspectives in the study of Latin American underdevelopment. *Comparative Politics* 10: 543-57.

Van de Walle, Nicholas. 2000. Africa in the world economy: Continued marginalization or re-engagement? In *Africa in world politics: The African state system in flux, 3d ed.* John W. Harbeson and Donald Rothchild, 263-285. Boulder, CO: Westview.

Van Maanen, John. 1979. The self, the situation, and the rules of interpersonal relations. In *Essays in interpersonal dynamics*, ed. Warren G. Bennis et al., Homewood, IL: Dorsey Press.

Van Maanen, John, and S. Barley. 1985. Cultural organization: Fragments of a theory. In *Organization culture*, 31-54, ed. Peter J. Frost, Larry F. Moore, Meryl R. Louis, Craig C. Lundberg, and Joanne Martin, Beverly Hills, CA: Sage.

Vengroff, Richard. 1976. *Botswana: Rural development in the shadow of apartheid*. Rutherford, NJ: Fairleigh Dickinson University Press.

_____. 1983. *Development administration at the local level: The case of Zaire*. Syracuse: Syracuse University Press.

_____. 1988. Policy reform and the assessment of management training needs in Africa: A comparative perspective. Paper presented at the annual meeting of the African Studies Association, Chicago, Illinois, 27-30 October.

_____. 1990. Rural development, policy reform, and the assessment of management training needs in Africa: A comparative perspective. *Public Administration Quarterly* 14: 353-375.

Vengroff, Richard, and Alan Johnston. 1984. *Decentralization, rural development, and mid-level development agents in Senegal: A report on training needs*. Lubbock, TX: Center for Applied and International Development Studies.

_____. 1985. *Senegal's rural councils decentralization and the implementation of rural development*. Lubbock, TX: Center for Applied and International Development Studies.

_____. 1987. Decentralization and the implementation of rural development in Senegal: The role of rural councils. *Public Administration and Development* 7: 273-288.

Vengroff, Richard, Mohammed Belhaj, and Momar Ndiaye. 1991. The nature of managerial work in the public sector: An African perspective. Public Administration and Development 11: 95-110.

Vengroff, Richard, and Ogwo J. Umeh. 1997. A comparative approach to the assessment of decentralization policy in developing countries. In *Policy analysis concepts and methods: An institutional and implementation focus,* ed. Derick Brinkerhoff, 141-158. Greenwich, CT: JAI Press.

Wallerstein, Immanuel. 1975. The present state of the debate on world inequality. In *World inequality: Origins and perspectives on the world systems,* ed. Immanuel Wallerstein, 12-28. Montreal: Black Rose Books.

Weber, Max. 1958. *The protestant ethic and the spirit of capitalism.* Translated by Talcott Parsons. New York: Charles Scribner's Sons.

Weick, Karl E. 1995. Sense-making in organizations. Thousand Oaks, CA: Sage.

_____. 1979. Cognitive processes in organizations. In *Research in organizational behavior,* ed. Barry M. Straw, and Larry C. Cummings, 41-74. Greenwich, CT: JAI Press.

Weidner, Edward W., ed. 1970. *Development administration in Asia.* Durham, NC: Duke University Press.

Weil, Frederick. 1989. The sources and structure of legitimation in Western democracies. *American Sociological Review* 54: 682-706.

Weinrich, Elaine. 1978. *Britain and the politics of Rhodesian independence.* London: Croom Helm.

Welch, Eric, and Wilson Wong. 1998. Public administration in a global context: Bridging the gaps of theory and practice between Western and non-Western nations. *Public Administration Review* 58: 40-49.

Werner, M. R. 1928. *Tammany hall.* Garden City, New York: Doubleday, Doran and Company, Inc.

Wharton, John W., and J.A. Worthley. 1983. A perspective on the challenge of public management: Environmental paradox and organizational culture. In *Public management: Public and private perspectives,* ed. James L. Perry and Kenneth L. Kraemer, 126-142. Palo Alto, CA: Mayfield Publishing.

White, Louise G. 1990. Policy reforms in sub-Saharan Africa. Studies in *Comparative International Development* 25: 24-42.

_____. 1987. *Creating opportunities for change.* Boulder, CO: Lynne Reinner.

Wildavsky, Aaron. 1987. Choosing preferences by constructing institutions. *American Political Science Review* 81: 3-23.

Wilkins, Alan L. 1983. Organizational stories as symbols which control the organization. In *Organizational symbolism,* ed. Louis R. Pondy, Peter J. Frost, Gareth Morgan, and Thomas C. Dandridge, 81-92. Greenwich, CT: JAI Press.

Williams, Clifton J. 1978. *Human behavior in organizations.* Dallas, TX: South-Western Publishing Co.

Williams, Geoffrey J. 1984. *Independent Zambia: A bibliography of social science.* Boston, MA: G.K. Hall.

Wilson, Woodrow. 1887. The study of administration. *Political Science Quarterly* 2 (June), Reprinted from Quarterly December, 1941D: 481-506.

World Bank. 1989. Strengthening local governments in sub-Saharan Africa. Washington, D.C.: World Bank, Economic Development Institute and the Africa Technical Department. *Policy Seminar Report No. 21.*

_____. 1983. *World Development Report.* New York: Oxford University Press.

World Bank Group. 2004. *World Development Indicators Database,* April 2004. New York: Oxford University Press
http://www.worldbank.org/data/countrydata/countrydata.html

Young, Crawford. 1982. *Ideology and development in Africa.* New Haven, CT: Yale University Press.

_____. 1999. The third wave of democratization in Africa. In *State, conflict, and democracy in Africa,* ed. Richard Joseph, 15-38. Boulder, CO: Lynne Rienner.

Yukl, Gary A. 1981. *Leadership in organizations.* Englewood Cliffs, NJ: Prentice-Hall.

Zander, Udo. 2002. When Muhammed goes to the mountain: Globalization, cathedrals of modernity and a new world order. In *Critical perspectives on internationalization,* ed. Virpi Havila, Mats Forsgren, and Hakan Hakansson, 153-177. Oxford: Elservier.

Zeleza, Paul Tiyambe, and Ezekiel Kalipeni, eds. 1999. *Sacred spaces and public quarrels.* Trenton, NJ: Africa World Press.

Zuern, Elke. 2000. The changing roles of civil society in African democratization processes. In *Consolidation of democracy in Africa: A view from the South,* ed. Hussein Solomon, and Ian Liebenberg, 95-138. Burlington, VT: Ashgate.

About the Authors

Ogwo Jombo Umeh is Professor and Chair of the Department of Public Affairs and Administration at California State University, East Bay. His research is in comparative and development public administration and focuses on sub-Saharan Africa, democratic governance, organizational management and public policy. His publications focus on comparative administration and democratic governance issues.

Greg Andranovich is Professor of Political Science at California State University, Los Angeles, where he teaches in the public administration program. His research is in urban and regional policy making, and comparative public administration; his publications focus on issues of economic growth and development and collaborative processes.

Index

 Also from Kumarian Press...

International Public Administration

Better Governance and Public Policy
Capacity Building for Democratic Renewal in Africa
Edited by Dele Olowu and Soumana Sako

Building Democratic Institutions: Governance Reform in Developing Countries
G. Shabbir Cheema

Governance, Administration & Development: Making the State Work
Mark Turner and David Hulme

Managing Policy Reform
Concepts and Tools for Decision-Makers in Developing Countries
Derick W. Brinkerhoff and Benjamin L. Crosby

Reinventing Government for the Twenty First Century
State Capacity in a Globalizing Society
Edited by Dennis A. Rondinelli and G. Shabbir Cheema

Humanitarianism, Civil Society, Peacebuilding

Aiding Violence: The Development Enterprise in Rwanda
Peter uvin

Creating a Better World: Interpreting Global Civil Society
Edited by Rupert Taylor

Globalization and Social Exclusion: A Transformationalist Perspective
Ronaldo Munck

Human Rights and Development
Peter Uvin

Nation-Building Unraveled? Aid, Peace and Justice in Afghanistan
Edited by Antonio Donini, Norah Niland and Karin Wermester

Ritual and Symbol in Peacebuilding
Lisa Schirch

The Charity of Nations: Humanitarian Action in a Calculating World
Ian Smillie and Larry Minear

Visit Kumarian Press at **www.kpbooks.com** or
call **toll-free 800.289.2664** for a complete catalog.

 Kumarian Press, located in Bloomfield, Connecticut, is a forward-looking, scholarly press that promotes active international engagement and an awareness of global connectedness.